THIRD PERSON

The Work of the Holy Spirit

John Peters

RIVER
PUBLISHING

River Publishing & Media Ltd
Bradbourne Stables
East Malling
Kent ME19 6DZ
United Kingdom

info@river-publishing.co.uk

Published in partnership with New Wine Trust

www.new-wine.org

ISBN 978-1-908393-69-2
Cover design by www.spiffingcovers.com
Printed by MBM Print SCS Ltd, Glasgow

Contents

Dedication

In memory of John Wimber.

Acknowledgements

With thanks to both David Ptyches and Barry Kissell,
who set such great examples to follow.

1
Talking About God as Spirit

It's difficult to talk about God in an adequate way and this is why the biblical authors employ a range of word pictures to stimulate our imagination. For instance, if we read that God is like a fortress, a fire, or a father, our hearts and minds have somewhere to go with this information. We can connect with these images and they stop us being too abstract about God – who is, of course, beyond our understanding.

But we hit up against a particular problem with the description of God as "Spirit". Many Christians refer to the Holy Spirit as "it". I find this rude. Have you ever grieved or quenched something impersonal, like a chair?

I didn't think so.

Whilst we have a frame of reference for God as Father and Son, this isn't true for the idea of God as Spirit. Here, the concept is difficult to set in an everyday context, and our word "spirit" is impersonal – hence the Spirit, many Christians and "it". However, the Spirit is the third person of the Trinity – the uniquely Christian description of God as three distinct persons who are nonetheless of one being. Clearly, we need special help to grasp what God as Spirit means.

The Hebrew word *ruach*, usually translated "spirit" can also mean "breath" and "wind". So, let's dive into the depths of this

Hebrew word. Apparently, it's onomatopoeic, so saying it out loud actually helps us capture a sense of the meaning.

Go on, give it a try.

God as breath

To say that God is breath is to connect him with life. When God created Adam, he breathed life into him, as a result of which he became a living being (Genesis 2:7). God is the one who breathes the breath of life into otherwise empty shells (our bodies) and brings them to life. We see this in the vision of the valley of the dry bones (Ezekiel 37). The bones only come to life when breath enters into them. So the image of God as breath suggests that he is the one who gives life.

At a personal level, we desperately need the life of the Spirit, whether we know it or not. If we don't drink enough water, our organs adapt to the little we do drink, but our brain function is affected. Similarly, we need to drink deeply of the Spirit because he brings every aspect of the Christian experience to life. He reveals Jesus to us, teaches us to pray, helps us to worship, to understand the Bible, and he transforms our lives.

At a corporate level, we should be entirely dependent on the life of the Spirit. A deeper experience of his breath in any church or area of ministry will transform what we are doing – even if things are going well.

At a national level, it is impossible to deny our need for the breath of God. Let's not pretend; this is a time of radical spiritual decline.

Today, only 2,000 teenagers attend church in the Dioceses of London and this is, allegedly, a rare example of a growing Anglican Diocese. But God is the same yesterday, today and forever and so this is a critical time to ask the Spirit to breathe upon us as never before.

God as wind

We have all, at one time or another, stopped to watch things being blown about by the wind. Whether it's that paper bag, that small child or the branches of that enormous tree, we gaze on in wonder. We also hear of violent wind-forces, tornadoes and hurricanes, and of the widespread destruction they wreak. It occurred to the Old Testament writers that you could liken the activity of God to the activity of the wind. This is another easy imagination stimulator; God is like the wind – a violent, unseen force that has a powerful impact upon people and situations. The thing is, the people of Israel had a wide range of experiences of wind upon which to draw.

Some fascinating information about near-eastern wind

Israel was bordered by the Mediterranean Sea on the west and barren deserts on the east. The east wind produced a mist of sand that destroyed vegetation and parched the land. These were winds of considerable force and impact. They would create sand storms that obliterated your view of the sun. The Old Testament writers saw in this a contrast between God's almighty power and the comparative fragility of his creation. *"The grass withers and the flowers fall because the breath of the Lord blows on them. Surely the people are like grass"* (Isaiah 40:7). Just as the devastating east wind destroyed natural vegetation, so God was understood to be able to destroy anything that stood against him or his people. Plants might grow and flourish, but they would surely be scorched by the blasting desert wind. So too might human empires of unimaginable force rise up, only to fall at the will of God.

The Babylonian Empire reached as far as Egypt, Arabia, Cyprus, Media and Persia at its peak. Israel had been carried off into captivity by this unstoppable force and no one could imagine how it could ever be diminished. However, Isaiah the prophet, writing during Israel's captivity in Babylon, foresaw that a time would come when even this mighty human force would bow before the wind of God.

He alone is infinite whilst all else is finite: *"The grass withers and the flowers fall, but the word of our God endures forever"* (Isaiah 40:8). Just as Roman and British empires have come and gone, so too will those of America and China, and also of any tyrant who currently oppresses people. When God's wind blows over them, they will be no more.

More wind!

...but this time western in direction and wholly different in character. The west winds blowing in from the sea brought rain to refresh the weary land in the winter and provided a highly welcome breeze in the summer. The Old Testament writers noted how these winds brought refreshment, much needed moisture or cool. And they argued that in the same way, God was able to refresh his people. The prophet Hosea says, *"Let us acknowledge the Lord; let us press on to acknowledge him. As surely as the sun rises, he will appear. He will come to us like the winter rains, like the spring rains that water the earth"* (6:3). If you had to travel through the heat of the desert, how fantastic it would have been to reach an oasis, a place of refreshment! During the long, hot journeys of life, the wind of the Spirit brings us refreshment.

Still more about wind!

Wind tends to be known by its effects as opposed to being something we know about in itself. If we really strained ourselves, we could say that wind is air molecules in high-speed motion, but where is the fun in that?

We prefer to talk about the wind in terms of what it does. The wind is whatever it is that is blowing that piece of paper about. The wind is what's making the leaves on the tree dance like that. Or indeed, the wind is what caused that tree to fall over. It can be easier to discuss the activity of God, as opposed to his character. We say, "It was God" who healed our friend, provided us with the money we needed or otherwise answered our prayer. What we really mean though is, "It was the activity of God", but nobody loves a pedant.

Alistair McGrath argues in his excellent book *Bridge Building* that this is how Jesus explains second birth into the Kingdom of God (John 3:3-8). Nicodemus appears to be wrestling with the question of Jesus' identity (v3). Jesus answers his primary question, the question behind the question, which is, "how can I be part of the Kingdom of God and therefore part of what God is doing?" (v3). Nicodemus doesn't understand the concept of a second birth into the Kingdom (v4). Jesus explains that everyone must be born twice; firstly, through the normal human birth process which we know about and can even study if we are totally mad or medical. Secondly, through a spiritual birth, which is mysterious and cannot be seen, but the effects of which we can nonetheless experience. You cannot see wind as such, but you can see its effects (v8). You cannot see spiritual birth into the Kingdom, but its effects are no less real.

Even more wind!

Ever seen the after-effects of a serious storm? I was staying with some friends in Texas and was asked to choose a DVD to entertain some children. I chose *Twister*, which I had not seen. The opening sequence featured a cow being taken up in a tornado. I didn't know that the family had its own tornado shelter because of the very real risk of such events. Several children started crying. This is why I am not allowed to supervise them.

Imagine you went for a careful stroll around the neighborhood the morning after a storm and discovered an uprooted tree. You wouldn't stop to ask yourself how this had happened — and yet it is a rather strange occurrence. How is it that infinitesimally small air molecules can uproot an enormous tree? After all, think about this: air is what you are breathing right now — yet it doesn't appear to be doing you any harm. I can imagine the movie trailer...

Return of the Killer Wind! Vicious wind molecules take a congregation by storm! Only a mild mannered local pastor can stand between the people and certain destruction. See forthcoming blockbuster, "Winds of worship – it's not a breeze."

Of course, we often go about daily life without thinking about the wind because it isn't blowing. But we could easily watch footage of the impact of the wind in various places around the world, almost at any given moment. The fact that the wind isn't especially active now doesn't mean that it didn't tear up a storm in the past, isn't doing so right now somewhere else, and won't do so again in the future. We can't get the wind under our tidy control because, *"the wind blows where it pleases. You can hear its sound but you cannot tell where it comes from or where it is going"* (John 3:8).

Looking back, I was converted at a very special time. John Wimber and his team from California were at their most influential and we saw great acts of power through their ministry. This gave an enormous confidence boost to the churches that were open to the Spirit and raised expectations of what God might do in the UK. People began to practice the model of ministry we still use, as described in this book. We gained experience in praying for healing and deliverance, receiving words of knowledge, and a much more intimate worship style was born. The movement of the Spirit known as "the Toronto blessing" brought another huge wave of power through the churches, even though there were some aspects of the theology and practice that might have been handled differently in retrospect. The current movement of the Spirit at Bethel in California is indebted to these prior works of power.

Why does the intensity of the Spirit's work appear to rise and fall? Well, the very unpredictability of the wind teaches us that God acts in ways that we do not fully understand and cannot dictate. There are times when God feels very real to us and we are able to discern what he is doing. But there are other times when he seems to be distant and it's hard to know what he wants us to do. But we never know when God is going to blow upon our lives again, filling us with renewed passion and supernatural power. If God has done it in the past, he is surely able to do it again. If he is doing it somewhere else, he can surely do it here. This is the logic of prayer: *If God has done it before or somewhere else, he can surely do it again, amongst us.*

One thing is certain: we need to be men and women of the Spirit. Without the breath of the Spirit there is no life, and without the wind of the Spirit there is neither power nor refreshment. The Spirit of God is our principal need, though not always our principal desire. And we should be profoundly grateful that Jesus says, *"How much more will the Father give the Holy Spirit to those who* [simply] *ask"* (Luke 11:11-13). My experience is that God meets those who seek him, who ask for the ongoing gift of the Spirit.

Anyone can but who is actually going to?

At the end of each chapter, I include a story written by someone who has experienced the power of the Spirit in St Mary's, the church I lead. Some of these stories are absolutely astonishing and I hope they inspire your faith as much as they have mine. By choosing these stories, I do not want to give a false impression of what our church is like! We have many problems and miracles do not happen every time the doors are open. I simply wish to make the point that any church that cultivates an openness to the Spirit will have wonderful stories to tell.

True story

"I was welcomed into a volatile and extremely traumatic family life with my father reciting, 'There is no God but Allah' into my ear. These words came to define my life. Every day I learned theology from Islamic scholars, fervently reciting and memorising the Qur'an in Arabic and English. By the age of 10, I embarked on my journey to become a certified Quranic scholar, subsequently committing 200 or 300 page books to memory in English, Urdu and Arabic.

As things deteriorated at home, my need for acceptance, affirmation and significance in the eyes of the distant Holy of Holy, Allah, led me to press further and further into Islam. Each day I read countless prayers, standing 5 to 7 times a day in congregational prayer, thanking Allah upon waking and invoking his name before falling asleep.

Yet... I knew buried deep inside me was a blasphemous thought – a thought that is forbidden in Islam. I couldn't shake the feeling that I had a perfect Father in Heaven and that I was a daughter of God.

But, bolstered by every conversation I had regarding faith, I felt confident that even John, the leader of the church, would never come close to challenging the truth of Islam. In fact, I boldly issued myself the task of defending Islamic theology and preventing the conversion of innocent randomers. So, my attendance on his cultish Life Course was mandatory! And it was there, as I carried out my duty to Allah, that Jesus called me. He used four moves that were out of my comfort zone and prohibited in Islam.

1) A GUY invited me to church. Socialising with a Christian man was massively dishonourable to my family.

2) The church he invited me to felt like home. This was the oddest thing because the mosque never felt this way. This was the first time in my life that I felt safe and loved.

3) And to really introduce himself in style, God spoke to me through a drunk woman. At a church social, a woman came up to me and shared what she thought God was saying to me. She revealed a secret known only to my most intimate friends and said, 'Jesus chooses you, you don't choose Jesus.' At this point, I was petrified – because this was the first time I'd seen a drunk person and also because small cracks were beginning to appear in my faith in Islam.

4) Was marvellous, in my opinion. On the Life Course weekend away, there was an opportunity to experience God. On the final

morning, Ben offered to pray for me, but I felt uncomfortable and refused. So instead he offered to pray in the name of Allah, to help me engage. I started crying. It was a flash at first, moments of awareness of God's love that left as soon as they appeared. What did it feel like? It was flipping amazing! Finally, I felt that God was responding to me. Seconds later, John offered to pray for me. Again, I experienced moments of awareness of God's love and had a desire to cry.

Upon returning home, I wanted to replicate the experience. I stood, opened my hands, ready to receive and prayed in the name of Allah and nothing happened. I tried again, but this time in the name of Jesus – and the same moments of awareness of God's love appeared. My faith in Islam crumbled. I was annoyed and hurt. I'd spent my whole life memorising rules, performing to reach the unreachable. What had I spent my whole life doing?

At this point I stopped going to church, knowing that, 'anyone who converts from Islam is an apostate and apostasy is punishable by death'. I needed time to think. But after just two weeks I realised I couldn't turn back. For the first time in my life, without understanding the rules and structure of the Church or the Bible, I believed in Jesus and felt responsive to God.

Keen to test his power, I started simply by praying, 'God, I really want to go to the Shard.' Two weeks later, a friend randomly invited me to dinner there. Because it worked, I decided to raise the stakes. I asked for a helicopter ride, something I had always wanted. A month later, a friend bought me a 'helicopter experience' for my birthday. In hindsight, I should have asked for a million pounds. I quickly realised that if Jesus can give me things I don't need, he will certainly intervene to save me from the difficulties of my life.

Since then, in many ways, my life has been transformed. I've let go of the fruitless striving, instead focusing on developing an intimate relationship with Jesus. After 22 years of chasing Allah, I finally feel content. I have a new best friend in Jesus who cares for me, who I can trust and who provides in remarkable ways."

2
The Spirit in the Old Testament

We have considered some issues raised by describing God as Spirit. When we look at what we can learn about the Spirit from the Old Testament alone, we have to concede that the picture is very underdeveloped. This underlines how much we need the teaching of the New Testament to complete and interpret what we read in the Old Testament. Although we accept the authority of both Testaments, the former must always be read in the light of the latter and not as though they are co-equal sources of information about God and his dealings with the world. Failure to do this leads to the development of weird and ultimately un-Christian beliefs. A very committed and gifted person has just left my church because we are not open to the view that in order to be a real Christian, you have to become Torah-observant.

The two Testaments aren't co-equal sources of information exactly because God was content to engage in a progressive revelation of his character and will for humankind, beginning in the Old but culminating in the New. For instance, the beatitude, *"Happy are those who smash the heads of your babies against rocks"* (Psalm 137:9) is hardly compatible with Jesus' teaching that we should pray for those who persecute us (Matthew 5:44)! The Psalmist obviously doesn't know what Jesus knows about the character of God.

Several key Christian beliefs or ethics are not known even by the main players on the Old Testament stage. For instance, Abraham, who uses the same name for God as he learnt in Mesopotamia, "El", thinks it's fine to pass off his wife as his sister to save his own skin – not once but twice (Genesis 12:20, 20:2). When Moses finally discovers God's name, it turns out to be, "I am who I am" – which doesn't actually tell him a whole heck of a lot. In many ways, the

God of the Old Testament remained beyond understanding. No image of him (or indeed of anything else in the creation) could be made (Exodus 20:4) and his name was too holy to be spoken out loud – a tradition still maintained by many Jews today.

There is no precedent in the Old Testament for the resurrection of the dead. Also, Satan, an entity whose malign influence is operative throughout the Gospels, is almost entirely absent from its pages. Furthermore, the Old Testament emphasis on the absolute importance of adhering to the Jewish law, or on the spiritual significance of the land of Israel, are of virtually no interest to the writers of the New Testament. Instead, we discover that:

- Jesus is the fulfilment of Old Testament Messianic hope, the Son of David (Matthew 1:1)
- He is the true temple (John 2:19)
- He is the new Moses (John 3:14)
- He is the fulfilment of the Law (Matthew 5;17)
- He is the fulfilment of the Prophets (Isaiah 53)

Jesus felt entirely free to both abrogate and to restate the heart of the law on his own authority. His teaching (and that of the other apostles) is therefore the interpretative key to a Christian understanding of the Old Testament.

So here are three surprising fun facts about the Spirit and the Old Testament

1) The Spirit is hardly ever connected with the creation. In all forms of ancient religion, what is truly spiritual can be discovered through the experience of nature. In Old Testament thought, the emphasis is on the transcendence of God; the Spirit is separate from the creation. In Genesis 1:2 we read that the Spirit was hovering over the waters whilst everything else lacked any form or shape.

2) The second surprise concerns the rarity of any mention of the Holy Spirit in the Old Testament. The New Testament mentions the Holy Spirit about 150 times more than the Old Testament.

3) The Spirit does not appear in the Old Testament as a divine person. He is rather seen as God's personal presence and intervention:

"...but the Egyptians are mere mortals and not God; and their horses are flesh and not spirit" (Isaiah 31:3).

Michael Green comments in, *I Believe in the Holy Spirit*:

"Here the prophet groups flesh and people together, God and Spirit. The Spirit is on God's side of reality – quite different from our side. And when the Spirit of the Lord is present with people, it means the gracious and personal intervention of God himself."

So the Spirit is part of the God equation, but he is more like the active power of the Lord as opposed to a distinct person in his own right. So what does the Old Testament tell us about the Spirit?

He is the Spirit of God

Although people in our culture want to describe aspects of their own experience of life as "spiritual", according to the Old Testament, the Spirit of God isn't an aspect of humanity any more than he is part of a river. The essence of human vitality is *nephesh* (belonging to humanity), whereas *ruach* or spirit is supernatural (belonging to God). Green observes, "the Spirit is not to be equated with any property in humankind, nor is it the stuff of which the world is made, a comprehensive life principle. No, the Old Testament insists that this powerful, mysterious Spirit belongs to God and to God alone." At this stage in God's revelation, it/the Spirit is essentially God at work in the history of Israel.

The Spirit is power beyond human control

We have already seen in maybe too much detail how the writers of the Old Testament helped to explain the work of the Spirit by reference to different winds. This stresses the experience of Israel that a largely unknowable but extremely powerful God had forcefully broken into their history. There wasn't a way of organising God's activity, or toning it down. This comes out clearly in the book of Judges. For instance, Gideon was a very ordinary, if not spiritually substandard man, until *"the Spirit of the Lord took possession of him"* (Judges 6:34). Then he became an unstoppable opponent of the Midiantes, the enemies of Israel who were making inappropriate use of that contemporary weapon of mass destruction, the camel.

We ask that we might be permitted to hear "the still small voice of God." But Elijah, who hears God speak that gently, has previously experienced the voice of God to be as powerful as an earthquake or a fire (1 Kings 19:12). To *only hear the still small voice* suggests that he is being returned to the norm, whereas he had known the extra-super norm. His depressed and exhausted request to be replaced as a prophet is granted right after this incident.

My point is that we should pray for the roaring wind, the all-consuming earthquake and the holy conflagration which leaves nothing but God.

This is Almighty God we are talking about – the one who created us, whose breath we breathe, who has conquered death for us and loves us with a passionate jealousy. This God can and does break into human lives, sometimes with huge and unexpected power.

The first time I asked the Spirit to come and touch a group of people, I was leading a week for teenagers. Our team had fasted three times and we had no idea just how powerful our time together was going to be. In fact, as we prayed prior to the first optional session, some members of the team collapsed under the power of the Spirit before our teenagers came into the room. We had to carry them out so as not to frighten or confuse the kids. The session was about worship and as we began to put into practice the simple teaching that had been given, people started to fall to the floor. I (rather unnecessarily) asked the Holy Spirit to come. It was as if someone started bowling people over as many people were powerfully touched by God. One French atheist, standing right at the back of the room and about the first to fall, wanted to know, "What was that?" Sometime later, I explained that "that" was the power of God. She had been deceived by her Christian parents who failed to mention that though they were paying for her to go to England, she would be attending a Christian holiday week. She also spoke no English, had only gone to the meeting because everyone else was going, and our conversations were through a translator. She had no frame of reference for what had happened. She asked me rather angrily, "Does this mean I have to become a Christian?"

Another teen ran screaming out of the room confessing his sins. He literally rolled around on the grass as though being tickled by the paw of a very big, invisible dog. The whole thing was so dramatic I thought that Jesus must be about to return. *I was young and foolish!*

This "possession" by the Spirit, having a dramatic encounter, is not the be all and end all of his work, but it can be the starting point, especially for unbelievers. I have noticed that those who have had an on-going, dramatic series of encounters with God have often gone on to be powerfully used by him. However, we need to remember that though some of these experiences may look disturbing, the effect is always beneficial and transformative.

The Spirit and the Word of God

Also, when the Spirit is at work, he wants to communicates with us. As Michael Green writes, "The wind or Spirit of the Lord is indeed power, but morally defined power, designed to communicate the will of God and bring his creation into conformity with it." That is why there is a frequent link in the Bible between the "Spirit of the Lord" and the "word of the Lord." It's why, when the word of the Lord is declared in the power of the Spirit, things happen. I was once speaking about the resurrection and I felt God tell me there was someone in the room with a neck problem. As I gave this word, someone listening to me was immediately healed. I believe this healing confirmed the word of the resurrection. The breath of the Lord inspires his word. *"By the word of the Lord were the heavens made and all the host of them by the breath of his mouth,"* says David in Psalm 33:6. *"The Spirit of the Lord speaks by me; his word is upon my tongue"* (2 Samuel 23:2).

Because there is a connection between the Spirit of God and the word of God, we need to leave space for God to speak, whether we are praying alone or worshipping with others – obviously through the Bible, but also through other inspired forms of communication. This is also why in the New Testament, there is a connection between being filled with the Spirit and speaking in tongues and prophesying. In the Old Testament, the message could take strange, mysterious forms, like dreams and visions. Hosea says that the prophet is supremely *"the man of the Spirit"* (9:7). Isaiah knows that his message is true because *"the Lord God sent me and his Spirit"* (48:16). This aspect of the prophetic inspiration of the Spirit is more fully developed in the New Testament, but suffice to say for now that we are being true to the biblical material when we encourage an openness to prophetic communication in all its forms.

The Spirit and leadership

Finally, there is a connection in the Old Testament between the Spirit and leadership. God gives his Spirit to his anointed king to equip him to lead his people. The prophet Samuel anoints Saul as king and the power of the Spirit comes upon him (1 Samuel 10:1). However, height (which appears to be have been the principal reason why he was chosen by the people as king), isn't all it's cracked up to be as a spiritual measuring stick. Saul the Tall disobeys God and is ultimately replaced by David – who may or not have been tall, but who did at least trust in the Lord. Samuel anoints David and we read, *"the Spirit of the Lord came mightily upon David from that day forward"* (1 Samuel 16:1-13).

Of course, the Old Testament record shows that subsequent kings ranged from shoddy to shocking with very few exceptions and consequently there wasn't much evidence of the anointing of the Spirit in their lives. The prophets, who had the incredibly depressing ministry of rebuking successive kings for their idolatry, hoped for something different. Would God raise up a worthy successor to David who wouldn't join his predecessors in disobedience, but would instead rule in the power of the Spirit? Isaiah longs for this:

"There shall come forth a shoot from the stump of Jesse and a branch shall grow out of his roots. And the Spirit of the Lord shall rest upon him." (Isaiah 11:1f)

It is important to note that the Spirit descends and remains on Jesus (John 1:32) and that God did not give his Spirit by measure or sparingly to him (John 3:24). Green comments, "In Jesus, we have the final embodiment of God's ideal ruler and he is fully equipped with an un-withdrawn endowment of the Holy Spirit."

In the Old Testament, the Spirit was only given to a few prophets, judges, kings, and to the occasional creative designer. But the Spirit of God was not for every Tom, Dick or Harriet in Israel. A promise like, *"My Spirit abides with you; fear not"* (Haggai 2:5) was given to the nation as a whole and not to anyone in particular. The Spirit came upon a few people to get the work of God done and rarely remained with them for very long. And yet Moses wished that *"all the Lord's people were prophets, that the Lord would put his Spirit upon them"* (Numbers 11:29). Ultimately, the prophetic hope for the last days was that this would come to pass: *"and afterwards, I shall pour out my Spirit on all people; your sons and daughters will prophesy and your old men shall dream dreams"* (Joel 2:28f).

Prophets like Jeremiah and Ezekiel looked for the day when God would strike a new deal with humanity. Although the Old Covenant was initiated by God, it still required the people of God to be true to their end of the bargain. *"If you obey my voice"* said God to Israel after the Exodus, *"and keep my covenant, you shall be my own possession amongst the peoples"* (Exodus 19:5). But there was the rub: they couldn't deliver on their end of the deal. Jeremiah foresees that God will find a way round this problem; he will enable his people to honour him by putting his own Spirt within them.

Here's Jeremiah's vision: *"'This is the covenant I will make with the people of Israel after that time,' declares the LORD. 'I will put my law in their mind and write it on their hearts. I will be their God and they will be my people. No longer will they teach their neighbour or say to one another, "Know the LORD," because they will all know me, from the least of them to the greatest,'"* (Jeremiah 31:31f).

Ezekiel explains that it will be the Spirit who will make this possible: *"A new heart will I give you and a new Spirit will I put within you and I will take out of you the heart of stone and give you a heart of flesh. **And I will put my Spirit within you and cause you to walk in my statutes**"* (36:25f).

There is a movement within the Old Testament away from a human attempt to keep the law, to the hope that a day would come when the Spirit's power would be available to make this possible.

True story

"We had travelled across the world to do a weekend of worship and teaching with a fledgling church plant in our network – one which wanted to create a culture of openness to the Spirit.

Getting the young pastor's newly assembled elder team "on board" was crucial and a dinner with a couple was arranged for the first night we were there. We were tired, they were sceptical, but John suggested we pray for them at the end of the meal.

There's no getting around it, it was awkward. They didn't really want to be prayed for in this way in our guest's living room and to be honest, I didn't really want to pray for them as I was so tired.

Anyway, I started praying for the wife and John prayed for the husband. Nothing was really happening, so we swapped. I looked at the husband and saw a picture of a scene from the movie *Hook* in which Robin William's character can't attend his son's baseball game because of work. In the movie, the son is ready to bat and is looking for his dad in the stands and can see that he hasn't made it.

Over the years, I have learnt to share things like this even if they don't make any sense to me, because there is a chance it will resonate with the person being prayed for. The risk of giving a picture that might mean nothing to someone is outweighed by the risk of not giving something that might change their life. Before I spoke, I asked God to show me more and sensed God say that I should tell the guy that although *his* dad had been absent at his baseball games in real life, his Heavenly Father had been there every time in the stands cheering him on.

I began to speak out the word and before I could get all the way through it, he fell to the floor and began rolling around, crying, then wailing, and after a short while, praying in tongues! This was quite a surprise as a few seconds earlier he was a conservative evangelical! We comforted his wife (who was obviously a bit worried about what we'd done to her husband) and continued to pray for him. Eventually he sat up against a table leg and just said, "So much love!" He explained that as a child he had been playing baseball (his team actually had the same name as the team in *Hook*) and that his dad hadn't made a game, which was unusual. After the game, he went home to find his dad at the door, bags packed. He told our friend that he couldn't be his dad any more and left. Our friend was nine. He described how, when I gave the word, it opened up the wound and he began to cry out to God for healing. As he did this, God began to flood the wound with his love and the reassurance that he had always been there.

This was a transformative experience of the Spirit for him personally, but also for his wife and for the young church as his story, which he bravely told in public the next night at our first meeting, created an openness that led to many more people encountering the Spirit."

3
The Spirit in the New Testament

By contrast, in the New Testament references to the Holy Spirit abound. From the beginning of Luke's gospel we discover that *"the Holy Spirit will come upon"* Mary and that *"the power of the Most High will overshadow"* her (Luke 1:35). When she meets Elizabeth, the mother of John the Baptist, *"the baby leapt in her womb and Elizabeth was filled with the Holy Spirit"* (Luke 1:41), which leads her to prophesy about Mary's child. Her husband *"was filled with the Holy Spirit and prophesied"* (1:67f).

This prepares us for the fact that the life and ministry of Jesus will be saturated with the Spirit's presence and power.

The Spirit descends upon Jesus at his baptism in the form of a dove (Mark 1:10). John the Baptist foresees that the baptism his cousin will bring will be infinitely more powerful than his own; it will be, *"with the Holy Spirit and fire"* (Mark 1:8). It is the Spirit who mysteriously leads Jesus off *"into the wilderness to be tempted by the devil"* (Mark 1:12-13). Emerging from this experience, Jesus begins his ministry in the power of the Spirit (Luke 4:14,18). He heals the sick (Mark 1:34), casts out demons (Matthew 12:28) and has revelations about people and situations by the power of the Spirit (Matthew 17:24-27). And he makes it clear that, *"by myself, I can do nothing"* (John 5:30).

Most of Jesus' own teaching about the Holy Spirit can be found in (John 14-16). Here we discover that the Holy Spirit is a "comforter" – or, in the Greek, "helper" or "counsellor" (14:16; 14:26; 15:26). He will come to the disciples to comfort/help/counsel them just as Jesus did when he was with them. The Holy Spirit is the *"Spirit of truth"* (14:17; 15:26; 16:13) and will lead them into a full understanding of Jesus' identity, purpose and teaching. The Father sends the Holy Spirit only at the Son's request (14:16) and in his name (14:26). Having been given to the disciples, he will remain with them (14:16), bringing Jesus's words to their remembrance (14:25-26) and helping them bear witness to him (15:27). Through their Spirit-empowered ministry, *"the world will be convinced of sin, righteousness, and judgment"* (16:8-11).

So in the Old Testament, the people of God had to rely upon just a few Spirit-anointed people (usually kings or prophets) who still bore all the hallmarks of human frailty. Although, in the Gospels, people sometimes liken Jesus to a king or a prophet because of the spiritual power he exercises, in fact there is no comparison between him and anyone who had gone before. In Jesus, we see the first fully Spirit-filled person. And that filling is without measure with the result that he performs extraordinary acts of power. He also uniquely promises that the gift of the Spirit will be given to all who believe in him.

After his resurrection, Jesus instructs his disciples to wait in Jerusalem because: *"you will be baptised with the Holy Spirit"* (Acts 1:4-5), a promise fulfilled on the Day of Pentecost (2:1-4). The Spirit overwhelms them and they speak *"in other tongues"* (2:4). Peter interprets this as the fulfilment of the prophetic hope of Joel: *"In the last days, God says, I will pour out my Spirit on all people"* (2:16-21). From then on, it becomes normal for new believers to receive the Holy Spirit at or around the time of their conversion as the Gospel spreads like an unstoppable fire out from Jerusalem to Samaria (Acts 8:15) and then to the first Gentiles (10:44-48). Saul receives the Spirit when the disciple Ananias lays hands on him three days after his conversion (9:17). A puzzling exception to the norm happens when a dozen or so disciples of John the Baptist (19:1-6) "believe", but don't receive the Spirit. Most likely they weren't truly converted and knew nothing about the Spirit until their encounter with Paul. After trusting in Christ and being baptized, they receive the Holy Spirit through the laying on of Paul's hands.

The religious authorities went to enormous lengths to have Jesus arrested and executed. It must have been deeply shocking to find his disciples performing miracles just as Jesus had done, with the same stunning impact upon the people. Of course, Jesus prepared his disciples for this, explaining *"everything"* about his ministry *"to them privately"* (Mark 4:34). He also sent them out on a trial ministry run with authority to preach, heal and cast out demons (Luke 10). So when Peter heals a crippled beggar (Acts 3), he does it exactly as his master would have done. And with explosive results: *"crowds gathered also from the towns around Jerusalem bringing their sick and those tormented by evil spirits and all of them were healed"* (Acts 5:16). This "summary statement" mirrors the description of Jesus' ministry (Matthew 4:23-25).

Even those set apart to wait upon tables in the early church needed to be *"full of the Spirit and wisdom"* (Acts 6:3). The apostles, faced with mounting opposition, spent no time praying for protection or trying to wrestle with principalities and powers, they simply asked for courage to carry on doing what they were already doing and *"the place where they were meeting was shaken. And they were filled with the Holy Spirit and spoke the word of God boldly"* (Act 4:31).

It becomes obvious that the Spirit is the real director of their mission. He leads Philip away from effective work amongst many to bear witness to one Ethiopian eunuch in the desert (8:29ff) – and then "transports" him back again! The inclusion of the Gentiles is clearly shown to be an initiative of the Spirt (10:19-20; 11:12). On the other hand, he prevents Paul from pursuing his plan to minister in particular regions (16:6-7). And he warns him of the dangers of going to Jerusalem (20:22-23). So just like Jesus, the disciples find that they can do astonishing things if the Spirit is directing them – and absolutely nothing if he isn't.

This surely sets a clear template for evangelism. We need the Spirit to empower and guide us.

What happened, then?

At what point did the church lose touch with the power of the Spirit? How have we subsequently settled for such powerlessness? This is surely the primary tragedy of church history, *unless this was God's will somehow?*

It's hard to see how it could be though, and indeed down the ages some people have continued to experience the power of the Spirit and see miracles, signs and wonders in their day.

The Spirit in Paul's letters

The Holy Spirit occupies a prominent place in the rest of the New Testament as well. Let's touch on the main Pauline contributions to our understanding of his work.

The Spirit lives within us (Romans 5:5)

To be a Christian is not simply to accept that certain propositions are true (such as, Jesus is Israel's Messiah), but rather to be indwelt by the Holy Spirit of truth himself. And Paul assumes that his readers have already experienced the Spirit for themselves as a result of his ministry of preaching and the laying on of hands, or that of others. For instance, the reason our *"hope does not disappoint"* is that *"the love of God has been poured out in our hearts through the Holy Spirit, who is given to us"* (Romans 5:5). By the term "heart," Paul refers to what a human being truly is, to his or her cognitive and volitional centre. The metaphor of "pouring out" communicates the idea of overflowing abundance. Believers do not naturally possess the Spirit by virtue of being human and made in the image of God, (reflecting the teaching of the Old Testament). Rather the Spirit is given to us as a gift from God who is above and beyond us. God pours out his overflowing love into our hearts by his Spirit. And this "proves" his saving intention towards us. Our present experience of the Spirit confirms our hope for a completion of the process of salvation currently going on in our lives. Elsewhere, Paul describes the gift of the Spirit as being like a "seal" or guarantee of all that is to come in the future, including our own resurrection from the dead (2 Corinthians 1:22).

We are now "in the Spirit" (Rom 8:9-11)

Here, Paul contrasts two mutually-exclusive modes of being: "in the Spirit" and "in the flesh". To be "in the Spirit" results from being indwelt by the Spirit: *"you are not in the flesh but in the Spirit, so long as the Spirit of God dwells in you"* (8:9a). A decisive change in our mode of being has been introduced by virtue of our conversion. We are no longer to define ourselves, or to behave, as though we are "in the flesh" when in fact, all believers are now "in the Spirit". Which means, having immediate access to the power of the Spirit who lives within us.

We are now part of a new body (1 Corinthians 12:12-13)

In explanation of his assertion that *"the body is one"* (12:12), Paul says, *"we were all baptised by one Spirit into one body."* The reception of one and the same Spirit means that all believers are included in one spiritual body. Just as the Corinthians had literally been *baptised* in water, so metaphorically, they were also *baptised* into the Spirit. This phrase is not meant to suggest a two-tier initiation into the Christian life; "baptism in the Spirit" is simply a metaphor Paul uses for conversion because he has been discussing water baptism. In the same verse, still speaking metaphorically, Paul says, *"we were given one Spirit to drink."* All believers have the same Spirit in them, just as everyone who drinks from the same cup has the same fluid substance within them.

We are all children of God (Galatians 4:6)

Paul says to the believers at Galatia that, *"God sent the Spirit of his Son into your hearts"* and that he then causes us to cry out *"Abba, Father"* (the Aramaic word for "daddy"). The fact that the Spirit dwells in our hearts as believers shows that we truly belong to him in the most intimate way possible, as his children. We then, are given the privilege of addressing him accordingly.

We can live to please God (Romans 8:1-9)

Believers are now empowered by the Spirit and not controlled by "the flesh" (the sinful nature). This is not a "nice to have" option, but a normative transformation. According to Paul, the purpose of God in sending his Son was *"to condemn sin in the flesh"* (8:3b) in order that the requirement of the law might be fulfilled in us (8:4a). In Romans 13:8-10 and Galatians 5:14 Paul defines love as the fulfilment of the law – as does Jesus in the Sermon on the Mount. We find that a new "law" is at work in us, freeing us from the old law of sin and death (8:2) and enabling us to love. The inclusion of the phrase *"in Christ Jesus"* (8:1), found everywhere in Paul's writings, denotes that this is only possible because of Christ who lives in us by his Spirit.

Paul contrasts *"those who are according to the flesh"* with *"those who are according to the Spirit"* (8:5). Believers are no longer helplessly subject to the desires of the flesh because we have access to the power of the Spirit. And as one popular ad went, "access takes the waiting out of wanting". But this is not a new code: "thou shalt follow the way of the Spirit". We can only live this out as we connect deeply with the Spirit who dwells within us, allowing him to do in and through us what we would not choose to do, left to ourselves. In other words, an on-going personal experience of the Spirit is crucial for any who wish to live the Christian life.

When Paul talks about *"walking in the Spirit"*, *"being led by the Spirit"* and *"living by the Spirit"* (e.g. Galatians 5:16-18), these are synonyms, denoting the process of depending on the power of the Spirit within us, as discussed above. Such "walking in the Spirit" will result in not fulfilling *"the desires of the flesh"* (5:16). The Spirit desires what is contrary to the flesh and the flesh desires what is contrary to the Spirit. In other words, the flesh and Spirit have an intractable antipathy towards each other.

There follows a list of "the works of flesh": *"sexual immorality, impurity, licentiousness, idolatry, sorcery, enmities, strife, jealousy, anger, quarrels, dissensions, factions, envy, drunkenness, carousing and similar things."* These works are the manifestations of the flesh. By contrast, to walk in, live by, be led by the Spirit leads to the production of "the fruit of the Spirit," which Paul lists in (5:22-23): *"love, joy, peace, patience, kindness, goodness, faith, gentleness and self-control."* Another way of expressing that this new principle of obedience is operative in us as believers is to say that we have *"crucified the flesh with its passions and desires"* (5:24). This is a metaphorical way of describing how the Spirit has rendered the "flesh" ineffective: by killing it. We need to constantly remind ourselves of this when we pray: *"I am no longer subject to this fleshly pattern of behaviour. Indeed, the prison door is open and I can walk out – in the power of the Spirit."* As Paul says, *"I can do all things through Christ who strengthens me"* (Philippians 4:13).

We are gifted by the Spirit (1 Corinthians 12, Romans 12)
According to Paul, the Spirit gives spiritual gifts to believers to be exercised for the benefit of the church. These gifts may or may not seem to be expressions of our character (generosity or showing mercy, by comparison with miraculous powers) but they are all supposed to be empowered by the Spirit.

Let's do the maths
- Jesus does nothing until the Holy Spirit comes upon him at this baptism.
- His ministry is then empowered and directed by the Holy Spirit.
- The apostles do nothing until the Holy Spirit comes upon them on the day of Pentecost.
- Their ministry is then empowered and directed by the Holy Spirit.

- According to Paul, the Christian life can only be lived out in the power of the Spirit. In fact, he is the person in whose dimension of life we experience God, if we experience God at all. He is the one who calls us to follow Jesus, convicts us of sin, teaches us to pray, helps us understand the Bible, changes us from the inside out and gives us gifts for service. No aspect of the Christian life can be truly lived out independently of the power of the Spirit.

- Many Christians claim to have experienced the power of the Spirit. They have seen people converted, the sick healed and bear witness to other miracles. In the period directly after the New Testament was written, the early church leaders tell us that everyone in the church got involved in healing and deliverance. Origen noted that Christians cast out demons, "merely by prayer and simple commands which the plainest person can use because for the most part it is people who can't read who do this work." He added that exorcism, "does not require the power and wisdom of those who are mighty in argument." Tertullian claimed that the noblest Christian life is to "exorcise demons, to perform cures and to live to God." Who knows how or why this confidence gradually ebbed away. Augustine, generally regarded as the greatest theologian of the first thousand years of church history, was initially taught that miracles had ceased with the apostles. When the sick came to him he sent them off to the shrine of St Stephen because it wasn't wrong to ask for healing, it just shouldn't be expected. He discovered though, that a large number of miracles were taking place at the shrine and he was so amazed by one story of the healing of a brother and sister from convulsive seizures during a service he was leading, that he had a re-think and ultimately began praying for people himself. He said, "I realised how many miracles were occurring in our own day and which were so like miracles of old and also how wrong it would be to allow the memory of these marvels of divine power to perish from among our people. It is only two years ago that the keeping of records began here in Hippo and already we have nearly seventy attested miracles."

There are innumerable accounts of moves of the Spirit throughout history

George Whitfield wrote of his participation in the famous revival in Cambuslang (1742): "Such a commotion surely was never heard of, especially at eleven at night. For about an hour and a half, there was such weeping, so many falling into deep distress and expressing it in various ways. Their cries and agonies were deeply affecting. Mr McCullough preached after I had ended, till past one in the morning and then could scarce persuade them to depart. All night in the fields might be heard the voice of prayer and praise."

John Wimber wrote, "When warm and cold fronts collide, violence ensues: thunder, lightning, rain or snow – even tornadoes and hurricanes. There is conflict and a resulting release of power. It is disorderly, messy and difficult to control."

Throughout the events known as the Great Awakening in America, unusual behavioural manifestations were the norm. I like this account from a "free thinker" of a meeting during the Kentucky revival of (1801): "The noise was like the roar of Niagara. The vast sea of human beings seemed to be agitated as if by a storm. Some of them were singing, others praying, some crying for mercy, whilst others were shouting vociferously. While witnessing these scenes a strange sensation such as I have never felt came over me. My heart beat tumultuously, my knees trembled, my lip quivered and I felt as though I must fall to the ground. Soon after I left and went into the woods and there I strove to rally and man up my courage."

After that, he went back in: "At one time I saw at least 500 swept down in a moment as if a battery of a thousand guns had been opened upon them and then immediately followed shrieks and shouts that rent the very heavens. I fled for the woods a second time and wished I'd stayed at home."

I came across this obscure account, which I also like: William Wade Harris was an African convert in Liberia. He began preaching in 1913. White missionaries told him that witchcraft was just a delusion. He knew that fetishes had spiritual power and so he rejected this idea and went his own way. He liked to burn any fetishes he could find. At one stage, pagan shrines would spontaneously burst into flames when he arrived in the villages to preach and the local priests would run away screaming. *Cool!*

Heidi Baker's modus operandi in establishing church plants today is as follows: go to a Muslim village, show a film about Jesus, heal a deaf person publicly and then preach the Gospel. *That will be why she's planted so many churches in Mozambique!*

I think we can dismiss out of hand the idea that people who bear witness to these things have been deceived by Satan. If Satan is involved, he is clearly defeating himself because these ministries involve bringing people to faith in Jesus and doing miracles in Jesus' name. I don't think Satan is either that nice or that complicated.

However, many Christians have not expected to experience the Spirit or the miraculous – and indeed, they haven't done so. Or they have been taught that the Spirit only works in specific ways now, through the exposition of Scripture or through the sacraments, shrines or saints – but not in other ways described in the New Testament.

I look at these realities in this way:

1. We only have one primary source of information about Jesus and how to follow him and it is the New Testament. As we have seen, it is full of the power of the Spirit.

2. Some people have clearly seen God move in power in their own day. They bear witness to signs and wonders in their own experience, performed in the name of Jesus. Although there are charlatans and exaggerators, I do not believe all these committed

Christians are lying.

3. Human nature resists the power of the Spirit, will do anything not to lose control, and is incorrigibly religious. It should therefore come as no surprise that many people have preferred various forms of Christian religion to the reality of relationship with Jesus, whether they know they are doing this or not. *

4. Because of the primary source and the witness of countless brothers and sisters that it is possible to live life in the power of the Spirit, we should choose to abandon a form of Christianity that is primarily about us or our tradition in favour of the real thing – which is about Jesus and the power of his Spirit.

To inspire us to do this or do this once again, we are going to consider the heart of what God in Christ has done for us as we seek to understand what happened on the Day of Pentecost in the next chapter.

True story

"During the past five years, I have undergone the most incredible emotional and spiritual transformation that has impacted all areas of my life. It's been entirely down to opening myself up to the person of the Holy Spirit.

I grew up in church, attending pretty much every week throughout my childhood. I knew and believed in God and his Son and I also knew about the Holy Spirit. But the church I went to didn't feel like a safe place. The leaders were very controlling and I always felt I had to perform or uphold some kind of unattainable moral standard.

When I moved to London, I continued to go to church and joined St Mary's, but the wounds of my previous church experience made me closed off. I found it hard to be open and vulnerable with people, even my close friends and my husband, because I felt that if anyone got close to me they would uncover my flaws, idiocy and failure.

This was my story for a long time. But one day it started to change. I believe God began to speak to me about living in a different reality: about trying to imagine a world where I was confident, where I didn't assume I'd fail and where I had true friendships. And I realised that that was what I wanted. I didn't want to be stuck anymore. I wanted to feel that I was free.

So when I came to church on Sundays, I started to ask God to meet me, to send his Holy Spirit to heal those emotional wounds and help me start to live in a different way. And it was amazing. I started a new job and I felt like a totally different person. I was confident, I stood up for myself, and other people took me seriously. I just knew God was with me in a very real way at work. At church, I found it so much easier to open up, I started to help on the Life Course, I started coming to the morning prayer meeting and I made loads of new friends.

I went to a conference about the Spirit at St Mary's. At the end, there was a time for ministry. It was really powerful; some people were crying, some were shaking, even screaming as their pain was being released by God. Though I was truly terrified to go forward because of my previous experience of 'ministry', I really felt God telling me to go and get prayer. So I went up to the front and said to him, 'Well, I'm here. I know I need to change, but I really don't want to cry, scream or fall over.' So the Holy Spirit came and met me on my terms. I didn't cry, I didn't scream and I didn't fall over, but after the ministry time, I did feel different. I knew God had started to heal me of those past church experiences and that he'd reaffirmed my identity.

That day marked the beginning of a new relationship with the Holy Spirit. I have been totally healed of the emotional scars from my previous church experience now and I feel that I carry the Holy Spirit with me wherever I go. This has been really evident at work where, because there is something different about me, I frequently get offers of new roles, promotions, chances to speak to my colleagues about my faith and chances to pray for them."

4
The Meaning of Pentecost

In its Jewish context, this festival celebrates the gift of the law and the first fruits of the harvest, but it is precious to the church because at Pentecost, the Holy Spirit was first poured out upon the disciples (Acts 2:1-14).

What are we to take from this? *#obvs*: if we want the Holy Spirit to come to us today, we need to meet in an upper room; which raises the question, do you have an upper room or not?

No, actually Pentecost is about God coming as close as possible.

It's a crucial chapter in the great love story God has been writing or re-writing from the beginning. To say that God is love (1 John 4:8) is to say that there must be an object for his love. An atheist dismissed this idea as merely a "linguistic argument" in a discussion with me. However, this is actually a theological argument derived from what the Bible tells us about the nature of God. No one merely loves – one loves *someone* or *something*. God loves us and people are sometimes aware of this, whether they go to church or not. But the fact that he has made us doesn't automatically mean that we can experience genuine connection with him.

You aren't necessarily "one" with something you make *like a jam tart, for instance*

In fact, we believe that God the Creator is distinct from what he has made. If an artist produces a painting, does he merge with the painting so that to know the painting is to know all that he is? Ultimately, there is more to a person than what they create, even if what they create expresses something *about* them. That's why we think those who search for the god within themselves are wasting their time. And why we aren't keen on reducing the divine to our highest human experience (the experience of love) because human love is not God. It is something wonderful that he has created for us to enjoy, *but he is more than a feeling.*

Also, harmonious connection between Creator and creation has been made impossible because we have torn the beautiful canvas God painted for our enjoyment, wounding it, him and each other in the process. God isn't just love; the Bible equally affirms that he is holy (1 Peter 1:16). Faced with our failure to live at peace with him and all the consequences that flow from that, he must either turn away from us, start from scratch, or cease to be true to himself. If you are forced to confront something you believe to be totally wrong – like child abuse – your sense of indignation either drives you to turn away from what you are hearing or, ideally, to work to obliterate it altogether. That is the logic of justice or holiness; it judges sin for what it is and seeks to overcome it. We only have a sense of justice because we are made in the image of a perfectly just God.

All the great saints of the Old Testament fell foul of the logic of holiness.

- Moses – who was not allowed to enter the promised land because he struck a rock when he should have spoken to it (Numbers 20:8-12).
- David – who was not allowed to build the temple because he had shed much blood (1 Chronicles 22:8).
- Elijah – whose request to be decommissioned was granted when he ran away from Jezebel (1 Kings 19:11-13).

In the Old Testament, we always come up against the problem that there is no adequate mediation between sinful humanity and holy God. Given this problem, it is astonishing that anyone managed to walk with God for any distance whatsoever, before their sinfulness undid them. Ultimately, when the holiness of God had been sufficiently offended by their inevitable failure (including Moses, "the meekest man that ever lived", and David, "a man after God's own heart"), each of them is judged and suffers the consequences.

The people are happy for Moses to meet with God on their behalf. They know that if *they* meet him they will surely die (Exodus 33:20) because of their sinfulness, his holiness and the problem of inadequately mediated God.

As the New Testament makes clear, relationship with God is not possible without the reconciliation of the problem of God's holiness and our sinfulness (Romans 3:21-26). At the cross, God achieves this reconciliation with no help from us, thank you very much.

"From the high heart of heaven comes the burning Lover's Son,

stretching wide his arms in welcome, to us living, disappearing ones." (This is the only line of poetry I have ever written!)

Where is the only safe place to stand during a jungle fire? A place upon which the fire has already fallen. The fire of God's holiness fell at the cross.

Pentecost, then, is the astonishing climax of the story of stories, of how God, who is distinct from his creation and wholly other than us in his holiness, has nevertheless found a way of coming as close as possible. He has made a way through the death and resurrection of his Son.

All who look to what God in Christ did are reconciled to their Creator, their failures are forgiven and they receive the gift of the Spirit (Romans 5:18, 8:1-2).

So, *question*: do you feel you are largely guessing at what God is like – as opposed to enjoying a relationship with him? Or do you try to earn his love by good behaviour, not appreciating that it can only be received as a gift (Romans 5:1-2)?

Pentecost is about the possibility of intimacy, something we are all deeply drawn to. The quest for true connection in our relationships and the pain that comes up when this quest is frustrated, is a large part of our story as human beings. Israel knew there was one God who had broken into their history and set them free from captivity. But, as I have mentioned, he seemed to remain largely above and beyond understanding. In the person of his Son though, God comes as near as breathing, as close as hands and feet, so that none need guess at what God is like.

But after Pentecost, God comes closer still.

Notice that the experience of the Spirit is totally overwhelming (Acts 2:1-4). His coming into their inner beings affects all their senses: they hear, feel, see and do something. It is as if they are ravished.

The angelic realm scoops up the fallen earth and gives it a good snog!

The disciples are left staggering and gibbering, speaking in tongues (2:4). This is a new means of intimate communion with the God who has come near and, of course, it must be later described as *"the language of angels"* (1 Corinthians 13:1).

The disciples are transformed in a moment from mere believers into ecstatic believing lovers.

Pentecost holds open the possibility that we can enjoy and delight in the love of God. I do not believe the experience of his love removes the need for connection with other people, but I suggest that it does transform what we are looking for from them. If we dwell in the love of God and accept that he delights in us, our natural need for affirmation is met to a significant extent. This doesn't mean the affirmation of people no longer matters, but we are no longer totally dependent on them for this. Having the love of God shed abroad in our hearts (Romans 5:5) is the essence of Pentecost and he gives us this experience of his love to inspire, empower and drive us forward.

Dutifully serving God is no substitute for his love.

Working for God as if we are employees totally misses the point.

So, *question*: has the love of God ever been shed abroad in your heart, or has it been a long, dry and exhausting time since that last happened?

The process by which we move away from God's love takes time and involves many decisions and circumstances. By contrast, the process of restoration is completed the moment we return. We see this in the wonderful parable of the Prodigal Son (Luke 15:11f). The father, who has been watching and waiting every day for the return of his son, is ready to pounce with the ring of sonship and the clothes of party central just as soon as the stinker appears over the horizon.

Such is the wonder of God's grace.

And this doesn't just apply to the moment of our conversion; we need to be restored multiple times in our Christian lives *because we are just that stupid.*

If Pentecost is all about relationship, then not surprisingly, it's going to be about communication too. Speaking in tongues is a language inspired by the Spirit to help us communicate with God. It is inchoate because it has to transcend the limitations of the language barrier. Sometimes we need to groan and moan. It's still communication, but it is more rough and ready and intuitive. Paul talks about the need to pray with his spirit and to pray with his mind (1 Corinthians 14:15); both are equally necessary.

God wants to communicate as a friend would, face to face. He wants us to know him, know what he is like as a person and to enjoy communicating with him. He also wants to communicate to and through us. With the Spirit on board, Peter is able to make sense of the author's book (2:14f). Joel predicted a time would come when anyone would be able to speak forth the things of God because one day it would be possible for anyone to have a relationship with him.

Now the Spirit lives in the heart of any who look to the Son.

How do we know when God is speaking? I describe the process as being like coming to recognise the colour red for someone with no experience of red, but who otherwise has full colour vision. God speaks through such things as Scripture, preaching, nature, visions, dreams, impressions, repeated phrases coming into our minds, a deep sense of knowing and good advice. God speaks to all his children and we are all faced with the task of learning how to respond to what he is saying and sometimes to communicate what we believe he is saying to others in a loving way. Here is a good example of how one Christian came to identify more clearly the voice of the Spirit:

"I arrived at St Mary's inexperienced in, but not averse to, the gifts of the Spirit. I thought they were super-spiritual, magical things that happened out of one's control e.g. like hearing an audible voice. I now realise just how 'normal' they seem to be, particularly gifts related to hearing from God. I find it's actually an idea that flashes across my mind or a 'feeling' about something. For instance, on two occasions, I have met people for just a few minutes but have 'known' that I'd meet them again and that we would become close friends. This actually happened and I met them both again at St Mary's. On another occasion, a friend was telling me about his plans to study medicine in Bulgaria, having been unemployed for a year. The thought flashed across my mind that he would actually come and work with me instead. This came to pass within a matter of weeks. Lastly, before going to a ministry conference in Sweden, I had a picture in my mind of a boy who felt acutely lonely. Before I travelled, someone gave me a word that there was someone I was specifically meant to pray for at this conference. Once there, I recognized the boy I had seen whilst praying. He actually came up to me and asked for prayer because he felt lonely. I prayed for him and told him that God had prepared me to meet him. He was very moved that God knew about his situation and cared for him so much. Amazing!"

We all have to learn to recognise his voice.

And this helps us to be led by the Spirit. In fact, if we are not led by the Spirit, what exactly is the point in calling ourselves believers in the living God? We might as well describe ourselves as "believers in an historical God limited to what he did in times past, who leaves us to make decisions about life for ourselves as best we can."

Though that would be a bit long...

Jesus did what his Father wanted him to do and in the light of Pentecost, so can we, by discerning what the Spirit is saying.

Question: To what extent is this your experience?

As I mentioned, we are sometimes asked to communicate what we think God is saying to someone else for their benefit. Probably the most important form of prophecy is something that confirms stuff we already know about our different callings or our identity in Christ. God in his kindness often affirms that we are who we hope we are in him, just when we need to be strengthened in that conviction through a prophetic word. Giving these kinds of words for the benefit of one another is one of our roles as a people of the Spirit.

Question: Has God used you in this way? Paul says we can all prophesy, of which more soon. Pentecost brings the experience of God, his love and his voice very near.

Don't let anyone take that away from you. And don't consider yourself to be disqualified.

God was pleased to pour out his Spirit on the disciples at Pentecost *despite everything,* not *because of* anything about them. Thankfully, we can all come as close as they did and on the same basis – the death and resurrection of Jesus.

That's it.

We turn from our life without Jesus, he forgives us for all that is past, and he gives us the gift of his Spirit.

From then on, we need to be filled with the Spirit and go on being filled (Ephesians 5:18) in order to live the Christian life.

This is what Pentecost means for us today.

Let's do the Trinity

I know that some Christians will think this is a bit naughty, but I want to argue that the concept of the Trinity is really an argument from experience. The experience of the people of Israel was that there was one God who had inexplicably, but very definitely, broken into their history and set them free. This act of deliverance (Exodus 12) is seared on their national consciousness and they are taught to confess: *"Hear O Israel; the Lord our God is one. You shall worship the Lord your God with all your heart, strength, soul and mind"* (Deuteronomy 6:4). And this created a monumental problem for the first disciples of Jesus. On the one hand, Jesus was clearly exactly like them in their humanity in that he looked, spoke and in many ways behaved just as they did. On the other hand, he was clearly nothing at all like them – not in his character, nor in the extraordinary things he could do; things that no mere human being could do. They can see that he is "Son of Man" – his usual self-designation – but although they are monotheists, they are forced to conclude that Jesus is divine: the Christ and the Son of God, based on their experience of him. They concluded that he was, whilst being fully human, also the same as the one God. After they received the Spirit on the Day of Pentecost, they found that the same God was still with them, speaking to them and empowering them to do the very works that Jesus did.

This further increased their experience and their God-formulation problem.

There are several crucial cultural characteristics the English have attempted to pass on to the world – like queuing, for instance, or talking about rain in a cheerful way. We instinctively know just how inappropriate it is to talk to a stranger in a lift and also why bus companies have created many, many seats – clearly, so that we can sit on our own without having to talk to a stranger (unless it is about queuing or the rain).

God has shown himself to have a flagrant and total disregard for our sensitivities.

His desire for intimacy with us is so overwhelming that he is like a person who will definitely talk to you in a lift or plonk themselves down on the seat next to you, spilling their shopping all over you and taking up more than their fair share of personal space – even though many other seats are actually totally free. God comes right in to live at the centre of our beings by his Spirit.

And so "the Trinity" is not a conceptual entity created from nothing at the Council of Nicaea hundreds of years after Jesus' death. It is an argument from the experience of Israel, the first disciples and all others ever since, that God comes closer and closer and closer.

So, who then is the Holy Spirit?

Not an atmosphere or a ghost or a special feeling. He is the third person of the Trinity, the one in whose dimension of life we experience God, the one who helps us live fully human lives and to fulfil our destiny upon the earth.

It is vital to understand his work since...

- Christianity is not merely a matter of church attendance. Going to church doesn't make you a Christian in the same way going to McDonald's doesn't make you a burger.
- Christianity is not a religion; indeed, as theologian Karl Barth observed, "religion is the height of our rebellion against God."
- Christianity is not a moral code in which we try really hard to live to please God. That's dead religion.
- Christianity is a living relationship in which we come to know and experience God in Christ by the power of his Spirit.

True story

"I am French and have Muslim parents. I was brought up to be a Muslim but became an agnostic. When my mother converted to Christianity, I thought she had gone crazy.

Then I came to London and a friend invited me to St Mary's. When I first came I was so broken; I had no hope, no faith and no love in life. As far as I was concerned, life had no meaning. I was also very closed off emotionally and that had various consequences. I had strong social anxiety, couldn't interact with people or look them in the eye and felt afraid and painfully shy. It seemed to me that my only companions at this time were sadness and loneliness.

I had never heard about the Holy Spirit or come across a church like St Mary's where everything felt so alive, full of love and joy. There was something about these people; they carried a light that attracted me even if, at the same time, I was scared.

The first time I experienced the Spirit was during a Sunday service. I went to the front of the church to receive prayer even though I wasn't a Christian. I was just curious, so I went with no expectations and left after one person prayed for me. In fact, I ran out of the church, crying and in desperate need of some fresh air! It was because the person who prayed for me spoke with real love. I felt I had to protect myself from such love. To hear that God loves me, to hear about his love and how precious I am to him, just hit me hard where it hurt. As a result, I didn't receive prayer again, though I felt strongly attracted to the services and kept going.

The second time I opened myself to the Spirit was during a week away with the church. We were invited to be still, open our hands and invite the Holy Spirit to come. I wanted to do this but found it too difficult and painful to open my hands. Then someone prayed for me and, again, it touched me right where it hurt. They said things that they couldn't possibly have known about me. Only God could have shown them what to pray for. All that night I couldn't sleep and kept crying as I released my past hurt. As I read the Gospel for the first time, I finally found peace and stillness.

I got baptised 6 months after that – on the one-year anniversary of my arrival in London. It was the most difficult but rewarding thing. I was so scared and stressed because I had to confront all of my fears about speaking in public and having all the attention on me. I never thought I would be able to speak the first word out loud, but somehow I managed with the strength of the Holy Spirit. This was the moment when I laid my past down before him, gave him my broken heart, my soul and my strength. I was actually desperate to know God more deeply and as a result he started to change me, breaking through the walls I had put up, and restoring me.

It is 3 years since then. If you met me today, you would never think that I used to be this shy girl, full of social anxiety or that I couldn't interact with people. Now I am the opposite, as the Spirit has transformed me. If you came into the church, I would welcome you, I would be all bubbly and would be able to make eye contact with you. You would not describe me as people used to, as "incredibly sad" or "frightened". Now people describe me as "joyful". Indeed, he turned my sadness into joy. You would probably see me dancing during the worship with my hands lifted in the air and you would never think that not long ago I couldn't sing or lift my hands because I was felt so ashamed and self-conscious. Every Sunday, you would also find me at the end of the service at the front of the church, either praying for others or receiving prayer. You wouldn't know that initially, I could only receive prayer briefly before having to run away. To pray for others was another battle of freedom, but again, his Spirit of power and love won me over.

If there is a church social, you will find me fully engaging in what is going on with no shame or fear and without trying to hide. I even do karaoke now, which is insane when I think back to where I have come from. My confidence comes from his Spirit who is alive in me. I have found that he has everything we need – transformation, healing, freedom, restoration, redemption, forgiveness, joy, boldness, fullness of life and miracles. I can say that I have found hope, faith, love and meaning in life through, with, and in him."

5
The Kingdom of God in the Old Testament

Pentecost is the culmination of the great story in which God comes as close to us as possible. But it's not just a story of intimacy and relationship, it's also one of purpose. After the Spirit descends upon Jesus, his powerful ministry of declaration and demonstration begins. After the Spirit falls upon the apostles, the same thing happens. In both cases, the Spirit comes to enable them to advance the Kingdom of God. And this is why the Spirit comes upon us too.

The Kingdom of God is quite simply the central tenet in Jesus' teaching: *"Repent, for the Kingdom of God is at hand,"* he announces as he travels through the towns and villages of Israel. Obviously, the Jewish people who actually heard Jesus preach had an understanding of what the term "the Kingdom of God" meant. So we ought to start with the Old Testament origins of this concept so we can understand our purpose.

Shockingly, whilst the term "Kingdom of God" is to be found all over the Gospels, the precise expression is used only once in the Old Testament. Some scholars assume the Kingdom is only a marginal element in Old Testament thought, even a foreign import from Canaanite religions, which expressed belief in a kingly deity. But the *Kingship of Yahweh* is a common theme and if we consider the main Old Testament context in which this term occurs we discover something really striking about God and his Kingdom that remains relevant for us today.

Although there are references to the kingship of God in the ancient book of Psalms and in the later book of Daniel, the most fruitful place for us to focus is the book of Chronicles. Here we discover just how closely connected *the Kingdom of God* is with *the person of David*. At the end of awful Saul's reign, the Chronicler tells us that, *"Yahweh transferred the Kingdom to David, son of Jesse"* (1

Chronicles 10:14) and similarly in (2 Chronicles 13:5) *"Yahweh, God of Israel, gave the Kingdom to David over Israel forever, both to him and his descendants."*

God will exercise his own kingship through David and his dynasty.

This doesn't mean that the earthly Kingdom of David and the transcendent Kingdom of God are one and the same. We are told repeatedly in the Old Testament that the rule and reign of God extend over everything. But God does specifically involve himself with this one particular earthly kingdom and through it, he works out his royal purposes.

When the ailing King David gathers the people of Israel together in preparation for the anointing of his son, Solomon, he says, *"Of all my sons – and Yahweh has given me many – he has chosen my son Solomon to sit on the throne of the Kingdom of Yahweh over Israel"* (1 Chronicles 28:5). The odd expression "throne of the Kingdom" suggests that the throne itself is a fixed symbol of the Kingdom. This expression is used again: *"Solomon sat on the throne of Yahweh as King in place of his father David"* (1 Chronicles 29:33). Also, the Queen of Sheba bears witness that, *"Yahweh has appointed you as King on his throne."* So *the throne of Yahweh* and *the Kingdom of Yahweh* are one and the same thing. This means that even symbols of David's Kingdom (his throne, the temple his son builds, the Ark of the Covenant) represent the Kingdom of God. Anyone related to him and anointed as King is destined to carry forward the purposes of the Kingdom. The Chronicler makes it clear that God chooses Solomon to sit on the earthly throne of God's kingdom to continue the Davidic dynasty as a mark of God's faithfulness to his promise and to build the temple.

This was a crucial time for God's kingdom upon the earth, hence the number of references of the kind I have drawn your attention to around this event.

Now David was by no means perfect but his son Solomon eventually worships other gods and things go downhill from there.

As successive Kings behave more and more unfaithfully, God continues to show his grace and remains committed to the Davidic covenant. Our next passage (2 Chronicles 13:8) contains the only Old Testament example of the simple phrase "Kingdom of Yahweh". Abijah, the truly crap King of Judah and grandson of Solomon, addresses the northern kingdom as they are about to attack him: *"Now you plan to show your strength against the Kingdom of Yahweh which is in the hands of David's descendants."* According to the book of Kings, Abijah, *"committed all the sins his father had done before him; his heart was not fully devoted to Yahweh his God as the heart of David had been"* (1 Kings 15:3), and yet God continues to entrust his Kingdom to him because of the promise relayed by prophet Nathan to King David: *"I will establish him in my house and my kingdom forever and his throne will be established forever"* (1 Chronicles 17:14). Abijah is "in" because he is part of the Davidic dynasty, although he is an unworthy representative.

So the Kingdom of God in the Old Testament is transcendent and universal, but it is also personally localised and focused in one person and his family, which produced more bad kings than good ones. The Chronicler brings together an absolute and eternal Kingdom and a personal, flawed, human one and the contrast stirs up the hope of another Son of David who could more faithfully represent the Kingdom.

Jesus' hearers were hoping for such a Saviour. It therefore comes as no surprise that Jesus is described as "the son of David" 17 times, understood by those who used it to mean "Messiah" or "Anointed one." Jesus is, by human lineage and divine commission, the true Son of David and therefore he brings the Kingdom with him in all its fullness.

But let's go back to David.

God calls him *"a man after his own heart"* (1 Samuel 13:14) and it is through this man that the Kingdom comes in the Old Testament. So what was it about him? His life was a rollercoaster of emotional highs and lows. He left us an example of passionate love for God and dozens of Psalms which are amongst the most beautiful and moving spiritual poetry ever written. His youth was frustrating, lived out in the shadows of his brothers, then constantly on the run from the jealous and awful King Saul. After he became the King of Israel, he engaged in almost constant warfare and was a great military conqueror. He killed Goliath, champion of the Philistines. He defeated many of Israel's enemies in battle. He refused to kill awful King Saul when he had the opportunity to do so. He had a deep friendship with Jonathan, Saul's son. However, he also committed adultery with Bathsheba, tried to cover up her pregnancy and then had her husband killed. He took a census of the people despite God's command to the contrary, presumably an expression of personal pride. He was lax and absent as a father, which had consequences for the development of his children and caused his final years to be marked by insecurity.

This has been a whistle-stop tour of a life.

What made David a man after God's heart, a person through whom the Kingdom of God could come, despite his human failings? Someone whose name Jesus took upon himself? I could draw attention to various qualities or attributes of David, but it seems to me that the defining moments of his life all involve expressions of faith and that this is the outstanding thing about him, *demonstrating that faith is the magic with God.*

David rises to prominence because he defeats Goliath, a giant Philistine, when he is little more than a boy. He challenged Israel to produce a champion for a "winner takes all" battle. The person who should have fought this kingdom battle was awful King Saul. But we are told that rather than trusting in God, he was *"dismayed and terrified"* (1 Samuel 17:11). Saul had been anointed by the prophet Samuel and could have fought for his nation, but he lacked faith. David, who by now has been anointed (16:13; something no one can understand), hears the same taunts and threats: *"This day I defy the ranks of Israel..."* but his response is totally different:

"Who is this uncircumcised Philistine that he should defy the armies of the living God?" (1 Samuel 17:26)

"Let no one lose heart on account of that Philistine, I will go and fight him," he declares, even though he is being repeatedly shushed by his older brothers. He has previous experience of battles against huge foes and he has won: *"The Lord who delivered me from the paw of the lion and the paw of the bear will deliver me from the hand of this Philistine"* (17:37).

But here is the crucial statement of faith:

"You come against me with sword, spear and javelin but I come against you in the name of the Lord Almighty, the God of the armies of Israel."

This is how he prevails – by his faith.

Those who advance the Kingdom fight and win battles and they win by trusting in the Lord their God. One triumph strengthens us for the next battle. God has used me to plant a few churches and I have often found strength, in the battles that have been involved, from previous battles won. If we are in Christ, then we are all sons and daughters of David. We have all been anointed by the Spirit and the Lord is therefore with each of us. Battles imply opposition and this comes from people who do not understand and from the devil. To say that you are signing up for the Kingdom is to say that you are signing up for war. And our battles aren't just external or spiritual, they are also internal and personal. We have to learn how to conqueror by faith the weaknesses of character that will otherwise be used to limit or defeat us. In various ways, David failed to do this and it was used against him.

Remember, David was old enough then because his faith was strong enough then. And so the Lord was with him.

It is absolutely normal to be dogged by conflict and controversy as we advance the Kingdom. David is harassed and assaulted by Saul for years. He does nothing to provoke this; the conflict arises entirely because Saul is paranoid. He is jealous of David's success and senses the anointing of the Spirit that is now upon David and no longer on him. His growing fear and hatred of David are unreasoning, unfair and based on nothing, in that David is wholly committed to honouring his King.

This leads us to the second incident in which David shows Kingdom-advancing faith.

Things get so bad with awful Saul that David has to go into hiding. But on two occasions he could have taken Saul's life. Humanly speaking, no one could have blamed him. The death of Saul would have solved some very real problems and maybe it was God's will? His men urged him on: *"This is the day the Lord spoke to you of when he said to you: 'I will give your enemy into your hands to do with as you wish'"* (1 Samuel 24:4). But he refuses to harm him when he has the chance, merely cutting off a corner of his robe to show that he has spared his life. His reasoning is as follows:

"The Lord forbid that I should do such a thing to my master, the Lord's anointed or lift my hand against him; for he is the anointed of the Lord." (24:5-6)

Saul, although he is awful, belongs to God. Those who advance the Kingdom will certainly suffer pain from friendly fire, but they should never inflict it. The eyes of faith see the calling and gifting of God upon other Christians. John Wimber was continually criticised for teaching about the Holy Spirit. It is to his credit that he set an example of never fighting fire with fire. As Christians, we are all on the same team and there are many implications of this for Kingdom-advancing people. For instance,

- don't be jealous of other anointed people
- don't try to usurp their position
- don't compare and grumble against God because he is using another anointed person
- do be grateful for every work of God expressed through other people

- do speak well of other gifted people
- do elevate others and help them to emerge
- do hold lightly to your position
- do pray for those who treat you badly or mistake your positive intentions for negative ones

This all requires faith.

Ultimately, David leads the nation in mourning for Saul when he takes his own life, *because he understands the tragedy that has been played out and takes no pleasure in another anointed person's disaster*. Win battles, don't fight your own team and, of course, follow David by worshipping in very little clothing...

....not really, this is optional.

Israel manages to lose the Ark of the Covenant and that's not good. But then they get it back and, after a bit of a palaver, it is returned to its rightful place. Much celebration ensues and we read that, *"David, wearing a linen ephod, danced before the Lord with all his might"* (2 Samuel 6:14). In fact, he went so far as to "leap" as well (16). He blessed the Lord in worship, the people with sweet foods (19) and he then went home to bless his family (20). Michal, the daughter of awful Saul, poured scorn upon him: *"how the king of Israel distinguished himself today, disrobing in the sight of the slave girls of his servants as any vulgar fellow would"* (20). David replied, *"It was before the Lord ... I will celebrate before the Lord. I will become more undignified than this and I will be humiliated in my own eyes."* In other words, worship is the most important thing – especially when the Lord has done something wonderful. His wholehearted worship isn't a cause for embarrassment, it sets an example for the people.

This is the leadership of faith.

Only those who worship the Lord above all things advance the Kingdom. Worship is the powerful language of faith. It declares emphatically,

- You are God and I am not
- You are almighty and I am not
- You are in control and I am not
- And I am H A P P Y about it!
- So much so that I will praise and worship God with gay abandon
- I don't even care what I look like or what anyone thinks of me as I do it.

What is the definition of an extremist? Someone who is a little more enthusiastic than you.

People of the Kingdom are worship crazy. It is in the context of worship that faith is expressed and restored, wounds are healed, wisdom and power are given. Kingdom people know this and those who are not, like Michal here, do not. I could go on: even the repentance of David after he has cocked up is an expression of faith. He might have made almighty mistakes, but he still belongs to the Almighty, so where else would he go than back into his arms?

In the next chapter, we consider the one Kingdom advancer who has no shadow side.

True story

"When I had just come to faith, I was on a Life weekend. We were praying for people on the Saturday afternoon after a talk on the Holy Spirit. I was completely new to this and still very timid.

I was standing watching when suddenly a dramatic picture came into my head of a man carrying a child out of a mound of rubble. I felt the picture was probably for someone in the room but didn't know what to do with it. A leader said, 'Just go and pray with that person and give them your picture.' I went up to him, prayed silently, but couldn't quite pluck up the courage to give him the picture.

The next day, I was sitting alone in my car getting ready to drive back to London when I heard a tap on the window. It was the guy I had had the picture for. 'Any chance of a lift?' As we drove off, I felt

God prompting me to give him the picture. This went on for some time until I finally mustered up all my courage and said, 'I know it's a bit odd, but I feel I need to tell you about something that came into my mind yesterday evening when we were praying. I think it's for you.' I then proceeded to describe what I had seen. I'd barely got to the end when I had to stop the car as he was crying. He then explained to me that the child in the picture was him and he spoke of his childhood in war-torn Lebanon. I was then able to pray for him and we drove on back to London.

A friend of mine became a Christian and joined the church. She was working as a tax lawyer in a large corporate environment in the city. She got on well with her work colleagues, but interaction was minimal and fairly formal as everyone busied themselves with their work. One morning, she noticed one of the women in the office was clearly in some discomfort. She had a skin disorder that seemed to be bothering her more than usual. She didn't know the woman very well, but she thought she heard God asking her to offer to pray for her. Not surprisingly, she was reluctant as this would come across as extremely unprofessional, if not plain wacky!

In spite of this, she could not shake the feeling that this is what she was being asked to do. Taking her courage in both hands, she went up to the woman and offered to pray for her.

She was surprised and relieved when the woman gratefully accepted. They agreed to meet at a nearby church during their lunch break. The woman explained that her whole body had been covered with skin irritations since childhood. My friend asked her whether she knew Jesus, to which the answer was 'no'. Would she like to know Jesus? 'Yes.' My friend then prayed that she would receive Jesus into her life and that God would heal her of the skin disorder.

The next morning, the woman came into the office and walked straight over to my friend's desk. 'I want to show you something.' They went into the corridor. She rolled up her sleeves so that she could see for herself the extraordinary thing God had done. Where previously her arms and her body were covered with irritating skin rashes, there was now no trace of them and her skin was like new! She had been completely healed.

Here's another story: I was looking to leave the job I'd been doing for a long time and so prayed every day about what to do next and the question I had for God was:

'What would you like me to do for you?'

For several months, I explored all sorts of noble and worthy causes, all of which involved doing something that I believed would please God. Then one day someone who'd never met me prayed for me and asked, 'Am I right in saying that you've been praying for the past few months about what to do next and that you've been asking God, "Lord, what is it you'd like me to do for you?"' Then she said, 'I believe God has a question for you and it is, "What is it *you* would like to do?"'

Initially I was amazed, but I immediately knew what I would like to do. I realised that I had been searching for a career move that would look good in God's eyes. In return, he told me that it didn't matter what I did — if I worked in the city, cleaned the streets or fed the poor. What he wanted was my heart. God showed me that he would love me whatever I did. What I really wanted to do was coach football for a living and for God to use me in that. And so that's what I did.

My wife and I were dance teachers and we noticed there were some people who seemed to 'collect' all the possible moves we taught, like trainspotters would collect train names. They would then string them together in all sorts of pre-determined sequences regardless of the music. Ah, yes the music...

These dancers never took the music into account. Instead they produced mechanical routines and their dancing never came alive.

By contrast, the dancers who caught our attention were those who imbibed the music. They might only use a few moves and even repeat them, but they were led by the music in such a way that these few moves always looked beautiful. Their performances had heart and passion instead of being constrained by the form.

We are not called to follow God in a mechanical, technically correct way. We are called to feel the passion of his music in our hearts and be led by his Spirit."

6
The Kingdom of God in the New Testament

It is Near (Mark 1:14-15)

Jesus' proclamation, *"The time has come; the Kingdom of God is near. Repent and believe the good news"* (Mark 1:14-15) is found in the most immediate, minimalist and direct Gospel. Mark's story is none other than that of *"Jesus Christ* (anointed one) *the Son of God"* (1) – a claim rarely made in direct speech in the text but assumed throughout. "The Gospel" (good news) of the coming of Jesus was predicted by the highly revered prophet Isaiah. He prophesied 700 years before that God would send a forerunner or messenger to help the people prepare for a new act of God by challenging them to turn from unrighteousness (3).

Many at the time of Jesus hoped that God would act on their behalf, but they didn't expect to be called to repentance themselves.

After all, they were the people of God.

They expected that God would establish his Kingdom and that everyone else would be brought to repentance. However, the preaching of wild and crazy John, with his funky clothing and eating habits (6) was so compelling that they even flocked into the desert to hear him (4). And were willing to engage in the public demonstration of repentance (baptism) normally reserved for Gentiles who wanted to convert to the faith of Israel (5). To receive the One (Jesus) announced by the messenger (John), the people would have to belong to God truly in heart, mind and soul and not merely by accident of birth. They would need to turn from anything in their lives that was currently spoiling their relationship with God. For the One who was to come was "much more powerful" than John the Baptist (7) and he would come offering a baptism in the Spirit.

BOOM!

Jesus appears and is baptised by John and the latter discerns that he is indeed the Longed-for One. Jesus himself tells us what happens at his baptism (10-11). This is a glimpse into the unseen foundations of Jesus' ministry, the answer to the question *how did Jesus do what he did?* as we shall discover.

Mark is minimalist, but if you want to fill in the gaps, other Gospel writers provide more information. The timeline is concertinaed but actually, after these events, months pass before Jesus starts to proclaim the message of the Kingdom. Before then, John is arrested after completing his preparatory role in the purposes of God when he even challenges the King to repent.

Whenever I have preached about the Kingdom of God I've always assumed *this will be exciting.*

On the contrary, it has always felt heavy going. I used to think this was because terms like, "Kingdom", "King", "rule and reign" are a bit removed from us culturally, or aren't that appealing these days and there may be something in that. But I have now come to a different conclusion about what the real problem is:

No one can discuss the Kingdom of God, even amongst those who believe in it, without stirring the primordial soup of human and spiritual darkness.

And that's what makes it heavy, man. Heavy soup, being stirred, with the spoon of the Lord. There is a conscious or unconscious spiritual lurch in the stomach as soon as we dip below the surface of things. And to talk about the Kingdom is to dip below the surface of things.

I mentioned in the last chapter that Kingdom people fight battles. In David's case, these were military battles. Here we see Jesus entering the spiritual fray. After 30 years of largely unremarkable existence, Jesus the liberator has come. *"For this reason the Son of God was revealed,"* says John, *"to destroy the works of the evil one"* (1 John 3:8). The kingdom of darkness has dominated for so long, taking countless sons of Adam and daughters of Eve captive. We are so familiar with the characters we meet in the Gospels, they are now sanitised and domesticated in our minds. They are figures in the landscape of our faith, not tragic examples of enslavement and victim-hood. We spend little or no time thinking about what life must have been like for these casualties of war.

Let me see if I can help with that.

Take the demonised man Jesus liberates in Capernaum (Mark 1:21f). What is it like to co-habit with an evil spirit? Would other people have known there was something wrong with you? Almost certainly, but they wouldn't have been able to do anything about it. They probably would have dismissed you as being mentally ill. Imagine the humiliation and public exposure as a demon screams out through you; to be the mouthpiece for a demon and remembered by everyone you know for that, forever.

Courtesy of modern media we are more aware of the physical horror of leprosy (Mark 1:40f). But did you know if you were a leper in those days you had to leave your family, your wife and children for a life of total rejection outside the community? Under no circumstances would you ever be allowed to touch another human before you died as your skin was eaten away. Let's hold that thought for a moment.

I sentence you to never touch or be touched by another person for the rest of your life.

You will also have to announce your pitiful, shuffling presence, shouting a warning: "Unclean ... unclean..." Imagine the astonishing symbolic power of Jesus *touching* you in order to heal, thereby making himself unclean according to the law. Going on from there, imagine the terror of falling ill without any access to medical care. Life would indeed have been nasty, short and brutish for many as a result of their diseases and, of course, for the poor of the earth it still is. No wonder when word got out that Jesus could heal, he was inundated with sick people (Mark 1:32, 37).

Now this is comparatively safe territory – not too much of a stomach lurch.

But we also hear that Jesus spent time with prostitutes. Let me increase the lurch factor. How degrading is it to be a prostitute? There may be some prostitutes who enter the profession because of the love of sex (a classic male fantasy). In reality, however, the vast majority are forced into it by exploitative or abusive men or drastic financial circumstances. And by the way, that is the main explanation for the porn industry as well. Forget the utter crap about women being empowered by becoming male sex objects. This lie, which some women participate in and spread around to other women like a disease, has primarily been engineered and enforced by men, driven by their depravity and an endless desire for money. And such men are laughing at every victim they create for the delectation of other men.

"The woman at the well" we call her in (John 4). She is a victim, the local slag that anyone can have. And like so many of the most notable captives of the kingdom of darkness, she is socially isolated, deprived of all the identity-affirming and healing connections we need to feel alive. She slinks along to the well in the heat of the day, because no one will be there. She is alone – to be toyed with by the one who comes to kill, steal and destroy.

Shunned and abandoned by the pure.

Let's not forget "the tax collector" of (Luke 19) who has given up everything for money. To be a tax collector for the Roman super-power, you had to be willing to collaborate with the enemy. Of course, you would do very well out it, as long as you were careful. Not that you could really leave your residence to spend it though, because if you did, you would be killed. And imagine the situations of desperate need that would confront you every day when your fellow Jews couldn't pay the tax.

• Imagine the power to rip parents away from their children

- Imagine the opportunities for the abuse of power
- Imagine dehumanising and being dehumanised

All for just a little bit more.

How many people will do anything for money, right now? Imagine Jesus spotting you in a tree, somehow knowing your name and inviting himself round to your house for tea.

No one went round to your house.

Let's not forget the victims of racism: the Samaritans, who no right-thinking Jew would ever associate with because of ethnicity. Imagine knowing that this person looking away from you in the street, or those children throwing stones with the encouragement of their parents, would rather die than acknowledge your existence, your common humanity. This still goes on everywhere.

Let's not forget the corrosive power of religious pride that causes Pharisees and Scribes to regard you as scum. You must have displeased God because you are poor or sick. Thank God that in my religious purity I am not like you. And as for women, I pray every day, if I am a Pharisee, thanking God that I'm not a gentile, a dog or a woman. Better that they are unseen and unheard. They might be the co-representatives of the image of God, but men surely represent his acceptable face whilst women rank below dogs. These darkly abusive attitudes are commonplace today.

"The time has come" says Jesus, *"the Kingdom of God is near. Repent and believe the good news."* The opportune time has arrived. It is always that time, time for Kingdom liberation, when Jesus is near.

He is gunning for every dimension of poverty, imprisonment, oppression, blindness and unhappiness you have ever known. And you know it. The primordial soup of our darkness is being stirred.

If it is time and the Kingdom is near, how do we receive it?

"Repent" means have a change of mind, either for the first time ever, or yet again, about Jesus. You enter into the Kingdom of God

not by being religious or moral or trying really hard. You enter in by acknowledging Jesus as Lord...

- not for a bit of spirituality,
- or as a helper when things are difficult,
- or as a vague friend you call on from time to time...

...But as the One for whom you have to leave everything and follow.

That truly requires a change of mind.

"Believe" means trust in or trust in again, not by a private transaction in church that can always be re-evaluated depending on how things work out, but like a person diving into the final space in a life boat. Get off this sinking ship and do it now! This is your last chance! Jump in with all your heart, soul, strength and mind.

We are all fifty shades of grey.

At least fifty and probably darker. Surely, it is better to go through life in the hands of the one artist who can colour us beautiful over time, if you are a son of Adam or a daughter of Eve? Simple as that. Why remain unarmed and unaware in a war you are in, whether you want to be or not; a war you cannot win.

Surely, it is better to take the hand of Jesus Christ, the Son of God and let him be your champion?

Surely it is better to let his compassion burn within you so that you can play a part in liberating captives and restoring dignity to other victims?

We are invited to extend the Kingdom of God with Jesus. This is what that that looks like:

- we have to be people who know how to repent
- we have to be people who know how to believe
- we have to be people who know how to be fishers of men and women

- we have to be people who know how to proclaim the Gospel of Jesus and demonstrate it in the power of the Spirit by healing the sick and casting out demons.

This is Kingdom life and everything else is playing at it. If this life isn't yet yours and you call yourself a Christian, do not rest until it is. I have written this book for you. Do not be neutralised by the enemy and do not sell yourself short, son or daughter of God.

Take up arms and fight.

True story

"I grew up in a conservative evangelical family, the grand-daughter of a Strict Baptist minister. For me, God has always been real, but not necessarily someone I wanted anything to do with. I'm not even sure I realised properly you could have relationship with him. I hated church most days, but it was filled with some lovely people. The crux of the matter was that I just couldn't see the point and though my head filled up with knowledge, my heart was rarely moved. The sacrifices I was being asked to make just weren't outweighed by any gain I could see. Often it seemed more about routine and appearances than anything real.

St Mary's changed everything. In my entire life, I'd only occasionally felt the touch of the Spirit whilst singing hymns from time to time. Suddenly, he was freely flowing and available. It went against everything I had been taught; the Spirit didn't move in these ways anymore and miracles were for the apostles. I had questions.

As I read through the New Testament and Acts these wonderful stories of Jesus suddenly started walking right off the page and speaking to me. It was as if, for all of those years, I hadn't really been reading what was written there at all.

As I went forward for prayer, the things I experienced and the words said over me were too powerful to ignore. I knew it wasn't me making my hands and legs tremble as I encountered the Spirit.

When I was growing up, I suffered with severe depression and felt suicidal many times. I lived my life thinking that the pain and emptiness was all there was. I once read a book called, *The Wind Singer*, in which a mosquito-like creature made its way into the body of a character in the book, turning him dark. That was how I felt – like something inside was consuming me and I had no control. I felt like a drain, sucking all the energy out of a room, just trying to fill the abyss in my own life. As a student, there were days when I couldn't even leave my bed.

It's been almost 4 years now since I felt that way. During a ministry session, people were praying for me about a month after I was converted. I can pinpoint the exact time the depression left me and it was as they prayed. I cried and shook and was bent over double as the Spirit did his delivering, freeing and redemptive work. The feeling inside me was so intensely powerful that I thought I was going to be sick. Then the depression was gone. I think this helps answer a big question: how can it be God when you can hear people crying or screaming in such obvious pain during times of prayer? Those things that were surfacing, all those lies I had believed, were what hurt. All the experiences God was releasing me from, they were what hurt. The thing is, those lies and memories and experiences weren't from God and my responses were to those, not to his loving touch. God, in that moment, was completely and utterly good as he set me free. Fully free, no relapses.

I then went away on the Life course weekend away. Up to that point I had pretty bad food intolerances. If I was not strict with my diet, I would find myself bent over on the floor in pain. Somebody gave a word of knowledge about God wanting to heal stomach problems. Someone prayed for me and I wouldn't say I felt anything particularly special, but I thought, "I'm going to test this." I'd really missed pizza. As I ate it, I waited for the warning signs. Hours later, there was still nothing. This was exciting! So the next day I got a burger and again I was completely fine. I decided to try some battered fish at work, much to the horror of my team (who were well aware of the side effects). It was just incredible and they couldn't quite believe it when I told them what had happened. As the weeks and months passed, I continued to be completely fine.

On the same weekend, I had a dream about a lady in purple encountering the Spirit. The next day, I saw her fall to the floor, completely overwhelmed by God as the dream played out before my eyes.

A Christian I had known at school was raising money to go and study somewhere in America. I felt prompted by the Spirit to give him most of my savings. I had barely spoken to him since our school days and I wasn't really sure if it was God speaking to me or not. But I came to the conclusion that it was. I didn't want my school friend to know it was from me, so I created a PayPal account under an alias to send the money. I had a little pray and chose the name Amanda King. I was following his Facebook fundraising page and to my amazement, the next day, he posted a story about how he had dreamt about a woman with that name giving him money! The name "Amanda" means "worthy of love" and I believe that God wasn't simply providing for this person, but also reminding him of how much he loved him.

Another friend had lost her wedding ring and put a Facebook post up and was clearly quite distressed about this. I asked Jesus where it was and he showed me a white chest of drawers and the ring caught down the side, by the runner. Assuming it was just my imagination, I said nothing. A week later we were queuing together and she started talking about her ring. Feeling a bit cautious, I asked if her chest of draws were white. She said they were. I then said, "I know you say you've looked everywhere, but have you looked down the side of the drawer, in the gap, by the runner?" She hadn't, but then found it exactly where the Spirit had shown me.

There have been so many times when I've prayed when God has allowed me to feel the love he has for specific people and it is so incredible, intense and beautiful. As I tell people they are often completely overwhelmed. I love to see people go from tears to laughter as they realise just how completely God knows them and how much he delights in them."

Spirit of the Lord was upon them. The Spirit descended on Jesus at his baptism (3:21). He performed extraordinary acts of power thereafter. Look at what happens in the synagogue in the next town just a few days later (4:31-37). Something is happening for those with eyes to see that makes sense of your experience of him, if you grew up with him.

But still, hard to take.

The Servant has been anointed with spiritual power for specific purposes. To proclaim a message of good news about liberation (18). Liberation from what? I bet you already know the answer, if you're there that day. I bet you know it with all the certainty of a terminal diagnosis. You must have felt, had you been there that day, as I mentioned in the previous chapter, that Jesus was gunning directly for the darkness and brokenness of your life, which he had surely seen over the years; *that he was looking right at you.*

That somehow he had the power to reveal it, bring you face to face with it and more – somehow deal with it?

How you must have wanted him and hated him at that moment.

2000 years have come and gone and nothing significant has changed. We haven't changed. Human nature is the same and hasn't evolved. We continue to be a mixture of good and bad, caught in a matrix of forces that lead to varying degrees of emptiness, guilt, captivity and blindness. In one week of ministry in LA, I prayed for people suffering because of depression, abortion, rape, child abuse, guilt, shame, abandonment, addiction and eating disorders.

All the usual things.

And many can confidently bear witness to the fact that Jesus' power to do what he speaks about hasn't changed either. During that time, we prayed for a lady who had suffered an assault. She spoke out in tongues and when she opened her eyes, her voice was restored and her colour vision returned as well.

I suppose the challenge for us is to recognise the humility of God who comes to us in the ordinariness of just another day, through normal flawed people and to choose to turn to him and not away from him, being willing to come out of our darkness and step into his light.

During that same week, I saw many receive new gifts from the Spirit, several were physically healed, more still emotionally because the church culture had not encouraged them to open themselves to God's power. One man was very cynical and so asked God to reveal the very situation on his mind to the person praying for him – me. I decided to go for it and God showed me that he felt very vulnerable, that it was as if someone had tried to steal something from him and I found myself praying for his family. He was struggling to come to terms with the fact that his daughter had a relationship with someone who might go to prison. He had just told his church leader that it felt as though someone had come into his family and stolen her away. Jesus is powerful and he continues to touch people's lives today.

How did Jesus do what he did?

Many Christians assume the answer is, "because he was the Son of God" and fail to take seriously the *Kenosis*, or self-emptying, that must have been inherent in the incarnation. When the Son of God took flesh, he "emptied himself" of some aspects of divinity e.g. being everywhere at once, knowing everything, being all powerful e.g. he grew in understanding (Luke 2:52), was astonished (Matthew 8:10), asked *"how many loaves?"* (Matthew 15:34) and why God had forsaken him? (Mark 15:34).

I think these are real questions.

He emptied himself in this way because these dimensions of divinity are incompatible with true humanity. They belong to what it means to be Creator as opposed to created and Jesus wanted to identify with us in so far as he could, not having been created and also being divine in nature. Notice, he did not lay aside sinless perfection – which is proper to his divinity.

74

We receive a glimpse of the unseen foundations of Jesus' life and ministry, how he did what he did, at his baptism where three things happened (Matthew 3:13-17).

1. He showed obedience

Jesus was baptised because this was the right thing to do. His favourite self-designation is "Son of Man," an expression he uses to emphasise his role as the suffering servant: *"The Son of Man came not to be served but to serve and give his life as a ransom for many"* (Matthew 20:28). He was under the authority of his Father" *"Yet not my will but yours be done"* (Matthew 26:39). There are many occasions when Jesus knows and does extraordinary things e.g. the fish and the coin (Matthew 17:27) and raising Lazarus (John 11:4), but he doesn't know or do these things independently of his Father: *"By myself, I can do nothing", "I only do what I see my Father doing", "I have shown you many great miracles from the Father"* (John 5:19, 30, 32). He didn't possess supernatural power independently of his Father: *"the power of the Lord was present to heal"* (Luke 5:17). This explains Jesus' emphasis on prayer. For him, intimate communion with his Father was the way of life, direction and obedience. His disciples noticed this and asked him to teach them to pray. He prayed before making important decisions – like the appointment of the twelve – and this opened the channels of revelation. For example, I believe that after a night of prayer he sees a group of fishermen and, as he looks at them, the Spirit shows him that they will be fishers of men – something he goes on to tell them.

So Jesus knew in general terms what his mission was, but relied on his Father for the specific details. He perfectly carried out his Father's will and was obedient even unto death on the cross.

2. He experienced the love of his Father

Jesus' ministry was always characterised by a deep compassion: he is moved with pity (Mark 1:41), has compassion on the crowd

(6:28) and heals the paralytic out of compassion (2:1f). He loves in this way because he knows himself to be loved (*"this is my beloved son with whom I am well pleased"*), an affirmation repeated at his transfiguration (Matthew 17:5). Jesus was very dangerous to the kingdom of darkness because he unequivocally knew that he was loved by his Father. He delighted in love and made love the guiding principle and force behind everything he did.

Evil has no answer to perfect love.

3. He was filled with the power of the Spirit
Without limit, in fact, in fulfilment of the long cherished hope that one day, God would put his Spirit upon someone and he would remain with him forever. Although miracles were and are done in the name of Jesus, the power comes from the Father.

What are Christians supposed to do?
Undeniably, Jesus taught his disciples to do what he did and they did it. They didn't do anything until the Spirit had come upon them, but thereafter they ministered to people just as Jesus did.

Let me whip us through the structure of the Gospel of Matthew.

- Jesus is the Son of God (various witnesses say so, like John the Baptist and God himself)
- There is a summary of the teaching that proves he was (the Sermon on Mount)
- And here are some incredible miracles that proves he was (some very big ones)
- Then the disciples are commissioned and sent out
- And then Jesus sets off to Jerusalem for the completion of his mission.
- At the end, we have the Great Commission (Matthew 28), *"teach them to obey everything I have commanded you"*, which presumably includes everything Jesus taught his disciples to do – healing and casting out demons included (Matthew 10).

Is there any basis for the view that whilst we generally follow Jesus (in forgiving or loving people) we don't need to do the supernatural stuff anymore? Is the existence of the New Testament enough with the record of what Jesus and the apostles did in times past? Some churches teach this, but it is a teaching without biblical authority.

The challenge of this book is as follows:

Let us commit or recommit ourselves to a biblical vision of ministry, if we claim to follow Jesus, keeping preaching the Gospel, healing the sick and casting out demons at the centre.

Why don't we? Well, some of us have been erroneously taught. And that is hard to shake because, as Rod Stewart acutely observed, "the first cut is the deepest". Also though, all aspects of Jesus' commission are offensive to the culture of which we are a part. Multi-faith dialogue is acceptable, but evangelism is not. Healing through the laying on of hands is regarded as a throwback to primitive superstition. Now we have hospitals. Belief in supernatural evil is defective because it represents a "pre-scientific" world-view. We have to battle against this all the time and a more aggressive secularist agenda has made this worse.

And the enemy is within. We are overly concerned about what people will think of us. We are affected by rational scepticism and quite frankly, aren't sure that we believe in the supernatural. We are very concerned not to "lose control" or "get carried away". We also prefer our truths to be demonstrable in a test-tube, but Christianity is not merely rational, it is super-rational. In fact, our faith is supernatural from start to finish, for goodness sake!

The supernatural is us.

True story

"A friend who had been diagnosed with brittle bone syndrome, fell over one day. She didn't think much of it as she often got injured. It gradually got worse though, and she started struggling to walk properly and so went to the hospital. They ran some scans and found she had broken her spine in six places and shattered her pelvis. Over time, the doctors took more scans and her pelvis began to look like tree roots because there were so many breaks/fractures. She had metal put in her back for her broken spine. It was decided that she needed surgery to fix her spine/pelvis, but that would mean she would be paraplegic, no longer having use of her legs. Having the surgery also came with a 70% chance of quadriplegia (total paralysis), becoming completely wheelchair-bound.

She then spent some time as an inpatient hospital due to not being able to walk and loss of feeling in both legs. A few weeks later, her numbness slightly improved and she was discharged and decided to go on the church student weekend away. There we prayed a lot for healing. On the Sunday night, she was filled with the Holy Spirit, laughing and feeling peaceful and received a real sense of hope that she might be healed and not in a wheelchair forever.

She went to the hospital on Monday after the weekend away for her regular scan slot. She received a call a couple of hours later from the hospital, asking her to come back. She had some more scans with different doctors, after which they sent her to Charing Cross in an ambulance for yet more scans. Her specialist arrived and ordered an emergency MRI, as the past two scans didn't make sense. The result of the MRI scans was that she no longer had a broken spine or a shattered pelvis. In fact, she was two inches taller, and her pelvis was a completely different shape.

She was completely healed.

She was born with a dysplastic hip, so her joint wasn't deep enough for the ball of her leg to fit. Now she had a perfect pelvis, which is clinically impossible. The doctors had zero frame of reference for this healing – they honestly believed they were looking at two different patient's scans!"

8
How Can We Do What Jesus Did?

Conversion

I was bored rigid by my childhood experience of the Church of England. Later, I studied Mark's Gospel in what was effectively a crash course in liberal theology. It was made clear to me that Jesus didn't actually perform miracles; the aim was to identify the symbolic meaning behind such stories as the feeding of the 5000 or walking on the water in an attempt to discover "the historical Jesus". This made sense to me at the time, not least because of the abject powerlessness of the Anglican churches I attended. Although I found it a bit painful to say goodbye to the person of Jesus, I became an agnostic and then an atheist.

I may have met Christians as a teenager, but they made no impression on me – apart from a Methodist minister who appeared in a school assembly. He spoke about Jesus in a totally different way and to this day I can still remember his face. Everyone in my class discussed God for the first and only time. By contrast, my parents, who had attended Anglican churches all their lives, had not managed to pick up any understanding of the Gospel and we never discussed such things.

I was very impressed with the lifestyle of the Christian students I met when I went to Oxford University. They were far more altruistic and peaceful in themselves than I was. But I thought I knew more about their faith than they did. Primarily, they must be weak and deluded people who needed an emotional crutch to make it through life, I thought. It didn't help that they couldn't answer my questions – but then I wasn't really listening anyway. Over about a year and half, I dipped my toe into the waters of spiritual debate, but just as quickly withdrew it. I met a lawyer who told me I had never considered the evidence for the resurrection. I tried to unload both barrels of Religious Studies O-level but it turned out that he was better informed than I was. I read a book he recommended that summarised the evidence and, as a law student, I found the case disturbingly compelling.

Ultimately, I was invited to hear Billy Graham speak during Mission England (1984).

This was when I first experienced the power of the Spirit.

As Billy preached, I lost consciousness of my surroundings and although I did not have a vision, I did become aware of the presence of a person – someone I had met before. Many years earlier, I had become aware of a presence whilst on a walk. There was an invitation to come and follow or to explore further, but I turned and walked the other way. Billy invited anyone who wanted to become a Christian to come to the front afterwards. I certainly wasn't going to do that, but I was aware of a force compelling me to leave my seat. So, ever responsive, I held tightly to my chair and waited for the strange feeling to pass, which it did.

I left the building feeling somewhat shaken. I then had an argument with the friend who had invited me, a conservative evangelical on his way to ordination. I guess he wasn't comfortable with arguing and suggested we pray together in my room. I hadn't prayed with anyone since childhood. As he prayed out loud, the presence I had experienced earlier filled my whole body. I shook and spoke in tongues and, in those moments, knew that I was completely known and loved.

From then on, I developed a massive desire to read the Bible, which I now felt sure had been written especially for me. I also found that I had an overwhelming need to pray, which I could happily do for hours. Shortly after that, I attended St Aldate's and had my first experience of a living church. I found myself crying throughout the services without feeling happy or sad – especially if the Gospel was going to be preached. And I wanted to talk to unbelievers about my new faith and this I did with great conviction, enthusiasm and insensitivity.

My new friends introduced me to Christian house parties for teenagers. A Pentecostal couple invited me to join their team and took me under their wing. The positive side of this was that within a year, I had seen people converted, healed and delivered. The negative side was that their very direct approach encouraged my own tendency towards unnecessary aggression and seeing things in a "black and white" kind of way. By the time they presented me with a tome of Pentecostal theology, I was unsettled (because I was getting negative feedback about some of my behaviour) and then concluded I couldn't agree with various beliefs that seemed to be central to Pentecostalism. In particular, that you had to get baptised as an adult, speak in tongues and have a "second experience" called baptism in the Spirit to be a real Christian.

Around this time John Wimber, the leader of the Vineyard Movement from California was speaking at conferences in the UK. I didn't actually attend these, though my friends did and told stories of amazing manifestations of the power of the Spirit. I simply read the books and listened to tapes of the teaching. And then I started to put the model of prayer that he taught, and that is described in this chapter, into practice. Here I discovered a theology I could embrace – in places corrected and enriched by evangelical charismatic theologians like David Watson and Michael Green. In general, though, here was a man who wanted to see God move in power whilst avoiding aspects of Pentecostal theology and practice I also found difficult. And most importantly, he really was seeing God move in power – so it wasn't just a theory.

Over the years, my two greatest joys have been preaching the Gospel to those who do not believe and practicing this model of ministry in the power of the Spirit. I can honestly say that I have seen God move in power in most continents, in many different people, in the very old and the very young. He has used me to heal the sick, cast out demons, give words of knowledge and prophecy.

I have seen the impact of this on many Christians with no real experience of the Spirt, but also on many non-Christians. Of course, in my personal life there have also been times of great brokenness too and I am still a very imperfect person.

My appeal has always been that if God can use someone like me in these ways, he can surely use someone like you. I have seen many come to believe this and even go on to plant churches in which ministry in the power of the Spirit is central. Some have seen God do far more than I have and they have taught others as well. It has been a great joy and privilege to see God work in these ways and a constant source of strength for my own faith.

The Model

It's not the perfection of our theology or the quality of our model that seems to matter that much to God. Rather, God looks upon our hearts and graciously honours our attempts to be faithful and obedient as we seek to follow him. Some of the things Christians have taught and done in the name of Jesus are frankly embarrassing to me, but I notice that God still uses the people who teach and do them.

What is he thinking?

On the other hand, let's not worry too much about them because we have problems of our own, don't we?

Broadly speaking, there are two extremes around today:

1. The Pentecostal approach to ministry, which can be flamboyant in style, stresses faith and the anointed individual. Most of my American friends deplore Christian TV and find it to be the main reason their friends want nothing to do with charismatics. In fact, in America I do not describe myself as a charismatic, because everyone thinks they know what that means. I must tell you though, that a desperate conservative evangelical friend of mine, with no prior experience of the Spirit, was healed of tendonitis by putting his

hand on the screen image of on evangelist's hand whilst he prayed for healing on the TV.

What is God doing?

The Pentecostal approach to ministry in the Spirit has the strength of approximating the way in which Jesus and the apostles ministered to people in the Gospels (Mark 2:11, Acts 3:6). There is also no doubt that in worldwide terms it is the Pentecostal church that has been truest to this dimension of Jesus' ministry. Also Jesus does talk a lot about faith, but I do not believe that is why God uses Pentecostals.

2. At the other extreme, we find liturgical models of prayer for healing. These are usually expressed in formal contexts, like church services. A downside here is that it's all a bit impersonal: you kneel at an alter rail and a priest anoints you with oil without even asking what you want prayer for. It's also increasingly uncommon for outsiders to find their way into a formal church context when they are in need of healing. I don't believe there is spiritual power in a priestly office in and of itself.

In one sense, thank goodness anyone is praying for people to be healed. On the other, in my opinion, there is an overemphasis in both approaches on the anointed person – either the healer or the priest – and not a biblical emphasis on the ministry of all believers. In other words, I don't believe that the ministry of the Spirt should be reserved for Super Spiritual Special Ones. Jesus was, of course, special, but his disciples certainly weren't and were probably chosen because they weren't.

This is the model taught by John Wimber all those years ago. I have pretty much adhered to it ever since, though the church in the UK has been subsequently influenced by Spirit-inspired movements and individuals who have advocated more Pentecostal theologies and practices after John's death. Whilst fully recognising that the power of God is being expressed through these ministries, I remain unconvinced that any have actually offered an improved model of ministry. And that is why I would still commend this particular approach to you.

Values

The values that lie behind Wimber's model are as follows:

- *Compassion:* the way we pray for people should above all demonstrate our love for the person we are praying for
- *The direction of the Spirit:* when we pray, we should seek to be guided by the Holy Spirit
- *Openness:* the way in which we pray should help people open themselves to the Holy Spirit

Step by step

Someone you know may have asked you to pray for them or you may be part of ministry team that is going to pray for people who come forward at a meeting or in a service. Of course, you may also feel prompted to offer to pray for someone outside of a church context, whether you know them or not.

Let's start with praying in church.

- Receive the person in a loving way. Interact with them in the way you would like someone to interact with you. Introduce yourself or simply go up to them and just start praying, noting any general direction that has already been given in the meeting. Sometimes, people are asked to come forward to make a particular response. Be aware of that – ask them if they are coming forward for that purpose.
- Explain what you want to do if you think there is any chance they have not been prayed for before. Remember, it is all about helping them open themselves and assuming they know what

to do when they don't doesn't help. Ask their permission to pray for them as you want to and describe what you want to do.

- Encourage them to open their hands in front of them, as a sign of openness to God and to close their eyes so they are not distracted. There is not inherent power in this and it's not a magic formula. However, since you are going to invite the Spirit to come and wait for a while, it is better if they express an openness to what God might want to do physically – as opposed to engaging you in a staring match with their arms crossed. Remember, openness is one of the values of the model.

- I say something like; "Hello, my name is John, what's your name? Are you used to being prayed for? You're not? Could I explain how I like to pray for people? In a moment, I suggest you open your hands in front of you, like you are going to receive a gift and close your eyes so you aren't distracted. But I would like you to pray first and then I'll add my prayers to yours. Are you used to praying out loud? You're not? That's fine, just pray in your head and nod when you've finished. Then I'll start praying for you out loud, basically to the effect that God will send his Spirit and hear your prayer. We are going to be here for a few minutes, so just do your best to open yourself to God and let me pray. Jesus says, *'How much more will the Father give the Holy Spirit to those who ask'* (Luke 11:13)."

It's all about making people feel safe and reassuring them that you are not going to do anything strange to them (stranger than God may do to them!). You aren't going to exploit their vulnerability, manipulate them in some way or emotionally abuse them. Some people can be very fearful that you might do this because of what they have heard or experienced previously.

- When they are in an attitude of prayer and have prayed then add your prayers in a really simple way. I always say, *"Come, Holy Spirit"* on the basis of (Luke 11:13), as above. If you are praying for a non-Christian this may lead to their first experience of the Spirit. If you are praying for a Christian, this is a shorthand way of asking God to come and do whatever he wants to do by his Spirit at this time. We aren't in any way suggesting that Christians haven't received or experienced the Spirit before.

- Pray out loud in a clear voice; avoid religious terminology, long prayers, shouting and prophetic words. The latter may be useful later.
- Take your time, and then take even more time than you feel you need to take, and then take even more time. Ask the Spirit to come and then, in your mind, go off and make a cup of tea.

Really, take your time!

The aim is to follow the Spirit. Your person needs time to open themselves to the Spirit, you need time to ask God what is happening and to look at the person you are praying for.

- Throw in a few more holding prayers like, "Thank you for what you are doing", "more power" or "thank you Holy Spirit that you are here." It's not about you and the accuracy of your prayers, it's about trying to track the activity of God when he comes and going with that. The initiative is not with us in any way. Christians regularly get in the way of what the Spirit would like to do by adding their long prayers, their best advice, their hugs and tissues etc.

Dial down.

- Even when people have come forward in response to something specific, that doesn't mean that God will be moving in that way. People often don't know what they really need prayer for. I will always pray for something they say they have come forward for, but often at the end.

- If you can see something happening e.g. they are crying, shaking, looking engaged in the process, bless what you can see. To bless is to "speak well of" in Greek. Our job is to speak well of what we can see the Spirit doing – even if we don't know what that is. There's nothing wrong with asking God to show you, but again I wouldn't leap in with this information.

- After a good while, ask your person what is happening. If they confirm what you can see or what God has shown you, say that. If you can tell that the Spirit is touching them, say that. People often simply need to be encouraged that the Spirit is touching them and that what they are experiencing is actually him at work.

- If a clearer sense of what the Spirit is doing has emerged after your conversation, pray again and bless what he is doing again. Often, more happens as we acknowledge that God is in fact at work.

- Stay with that one person until they open their eyes or you have done as much as you feel you can do. Then move on in a kind way.

- Don't feel stuck with one person – it's fine to move around and pray for others.

- Know when to ask for help. This would be when something is happening you don't understand or have no previous experience of e.g. uncontrollable screaming. It is common for very deep pain to come up during these times, but if you haven't seen that before it can be quite disconcerting.

- It's fine to pray in pairs so that A learns from B, who has more experience.

- Assume you will pray for the same sex, but since Jesus ministered to both sexes I'm not really sure we can impose laws about this.

Churches like to though.

Nevertheless, you certainly need to be wise, and entirely appropriate in what you say and do if you are going to minister to someone of the opposite sex. I would never do this ministry in a room on my own with someone of the opposite sex.

- Always wear a badge if you are part of a ministry team so that there is accountability if someone complains for any reason.
- Cut out any weird behavior; try and be a normal human being to a normal human being. Don't put your hand in the air to conduct unseen spiritual electricity. If the Spirit is touching you and you are manifesting his presence, get prayer yourself and stop praying.
- Try to avoid all Christian jargon.
- The time for giving prophetic words is later in the process. Initially, it is all about helping people open themselves. If I think God has shown me something, I will ask my person if anything I prayed particularly spoke to them. I might say, "I found myself praying for this/that. Did you find that relevant to where you are at?" If it is, then I would say what I have seen or felt. Otherwise, I would drop it, in favour of further discussion or prayer about what they are actually experiencing and talk about it afterwards.
- The determining factor is what you can see the Spirit doing and ideally what they tell you the Spirit is doing. Unless your sense of this is the same as the above, I would leave it. Christians can cause people to close down by engaging them in a long conversation about the prophetic word they feel they have when its only mildly relevant to what God is doing now. Not that I'm against prophecy!

The sorts of things that happen

- There are no rules and really, anything can happen! Sometimes, it looks quite funny, but it will probably be inappropriate to laugh. Whilst more private people can find it hard to open themselves, sometimes God just breaks in. Sometimes quite open people don't appear to experience very much. Never tell people what they are going to experience and do engage with what they tell you their actual experience has been. Even if it is disappointing. Say, "Well, we invited the Spirit to come and I believe that means he has come. You did your best to open yourself and we can always pray again."

- Never blame them or give them a reason to think they have failed.
- There are times of more and less power and the latter are very trying.
- There are more and less open people, cultures and Christian traditions; the latter can be trying too.
- It is common to start in one place and end up somewhere else, e.g. with someone asking for prayer for an illness when actually, the physical illness has an emotional cause.
- Some responses are very dramatic, e.g. to painful memories that are surfacing, or being filled with the Spirit for the first time, or power encounters with demons. None of these are new. All the great revivalists witnessed excessive emotional and unusual physical states in people they preached to or prayed for. It is fair to say that in the UK we have sometimes seen dramatic responses like this since Wimber first came. Not that his arrival signalled the beginning of the work of the Spirit in the UK.
- Ministry often provokes angry and bitter reactions from other Christians or religious people. Here's an extract from Wesley's journal: "A Quaker who stood by was not a little displeased at the dissimulation of these creatures and was biting his lips and knitting his brows when he dropped as if thunderstruck. The agony in him was terrible to behold – he cried aloud, 'Now I

know that you are a prophet of the Lord.'"

- We do not want to psychologically induce experiences. We don't want to encourage attention-seeking behaviour and we don't want to confuse the work of the Spirit with the activity of demons. It can take a while to work out which of these is actually happening. But in general, we don't need to worry about any of this.
- Instead, we need to pray for as many people as possible because of the extraordinary potential for transformation and healing that comes to people when they open themselves to the power of God.
- It is sometimes said that God is a God of peace and of order and that our services and experiences should reflect this. However, the disciples of Jesus had dramatic experiences of the Spirit in Acts 2 and 4. God does want us to come to a place of peace in our lives, but often the process by which this happens is somewhat disorderly.
- The English are not the measuring stick of emotional normality.

Common manifestations

- Shaking and trembling in the whole or part of someone's body. This is usually associated with empowerment, but if it is violent, could be indicative of pain surfacing or occasionally something demonic manifesting (Isaiah 66:3, Matthew 28:4).
- Falling: this has been a very common experience throughout church history. Some experience profound transformation and a few emerge afterwards totally unchanged. There is no great advantage to falling. Indeed, dramatic encounters may be God's rebuke. What he wants is simple co-operation; if he doesn't get it, there may be drama.
- There is nothing to gain from pushing people over or encouraging them to fall. If people are staggering around trying not to fall, I tell them that I will catch them if they do

(Daniel 8:17, Acts 9:4).

- Drunkenness: a spiritual state resembling intoxication. Some experience a euphoric feeling often associated with the love of God being shed abroad in their heart. Some experience a feeling of heaviness and inability to speak or walk properly (Acts 2:15), sometimes for hours. That's always quite amusing to see.

- Bodily writhings or distortions of the face: this can be the result of inner conflict or suppressed hurt surfacing. It may be demonic if accompanied by such delights as hissing, blasphemy or vomiting (Mark 9:2).

- Laughing and crying: this can be brief and light or episodic and carrying on for a period. These are both connected with emotional release and may be evidence of healing being received or needed.

- Praise: may continue for hours, especially when a new gift of tongues has been received or new anointing of the Spirit is being given.

- Less obvious but common manifestations include: slight trembling, fluttering eyelids, deep breathing, a feeling of weight on the hands, an oil-like substance on the hands or head, or wind blowing over them. These are first signs of the Spirit's presence. As we bless what we see God doing, often more happens. John Wimber observed, "This is a fundamental principle for effective prayer; honour what the Lord is doing and he will usually do more."

- Sometimes people have very obvious encounters with the Spirit, but seem to be disassociated from what is happening and deny that anything happened – even though you can see that it did!

- Sometimes people do their best to open themselves and feel disappointed when nothing happens. Usually when people say "nothing happened" they are mistaken. What they are experiencing is their own pain, not what they were hoping to experience. Imagine a person is like a cup. If their cup is full of pain, when the Spirit comes he will touch it and what is already inside will start to rise to the surface. The aim is to have them tell you what is the cause of their pain and pray into that.

- Sometimes people need several attempts before they are comfortable enough to truly open themselves and there is nothing we can do about that, except make sure that they feel loved and reassured that this is normal and they can always give it another go.

Conclusions

Observable responses to the Spirit's presence are important indicators of what God is doing, though they aren't a guarantee of healing and we should never proclaim that someone has been healed. If they have, they can tell us.

But the outward things aren't the most important unless we are praying for physical healing. They are like knee-jerk spasms of the body in response to the presence of the Spirit. God is primarily concerned with renewing and changing our inner beings, something we can't see. People often experience a sense of being loved by God, his peace or his voice when the Spirit comes. *This is what really matters.*

How to be more powerfully used by God than you are now

- Jesus was perfectly obedient to his Father in his life and in his ministry.
- Jesus perfectly received and gave out of his Father's love.
- Jesus perfectly received and gave out the power of the Spirit.

This will never be perfectly true of us.

Do not believe anyone who tells you that it is possible for you to be perfect this side of eternity. This side of eternity, all of us will fail to be obedient to God, we will fail to connect properly with our Father and, far from receiving the Spirit's power, we shall sometimes grieve him. We all needed to be saved for a reason and until the Lord returns, even the most committed amongst us are going to be no more or less than a mixed bag.

This is the sense in which Jesus is an unattainable model for us.

At his baptism, we glimpse the unseen foundations of his life (Matthew 3:13-17). There, he did what was right, he was affirmed by his Father and the Spirt came upon him. But Jesus went on to always do what was right. He dwelt in an unbroken communion of love with his Father and he was filled by the Spirit without limit.

However, if we wish to grow in effectiveness in ministry, the way to do so is the same. In so far as we grow in obedience, dwell in the experience of the Father's love, and are filled with the Spirit, we shall see a measure of ministry in the power of the Spirit if we pray for people.

It's all about the unseen foundations, just as it was for Jesus. If we want to do what Jesus did, we need to strengthen what is unseen but crucial in our lives. As God has demonstrated repeatedly by the way he chooses to use all sorts of people, these things are more important to him than correct theology, a sensible model or a good character – though these are all desirable.

For instance,

- I believe the Spirit prompts us to do and say things all the time. If we receive a prompting but don't take any action, we disobey the Spirit. This doesn't mean that God will no longer love us or that he won't give us further opportunities. On the contrary, God's grace goes on and on and on. However, until we start to respond by faith to his promptings, we can't develop a greater experience of what his direction is like. He waits for us to trust him and the reward for doing so is growing in spiritual confidence. This is essential to ministry because it is all about learning to discern what the Spirit is saying and doing and responding to this.

- If we fail to deal with something in our lives that the Spirit is convicting us of, God will still love us and his grace will go and on and on. But when we keep on sinning in an area of our lives, we build up walls of guilt and shame and our head goes down. This means we feel less confident to look into the face of our Father and dwell in his love. This means that over time, our identity as a son or daughter becomes shaky. This means we are less likely to open ourselves to the power of the Spirit and be used by him.

This is a vicious circle engineered by our enemy, the devil, to take us out of action.

When we confess our sin, we are restored to the Father, we look into his face again without shame, he re-confirms our identity as a son or a daughter, the Spirit comes upon us again and before very long we start to focus out towards others, out beyond the narrow confines of our own failure.

If we do not believe that God the Father loves us it is very hard to trust that he wants to use us. Dwelling in the love of the Father affirms our identity as a son or a daughter and it is only sons and daughters who minister in the power of the Spirit. Those who believe themselves to be unwanted, unloved, spiritual orphans do not.

You are not who you think you are. You are who you think the most significant people in your life think you are. If the most significant person in your life is God and you believe you are dearly loved by him as his child, this will have a massive impact on your sense of identity and capacity to follow the Holy Spirit.

This is why it is crucial to distinguish your own father from God the Father and to learn to treat God as the inexpressible giver of unconditional love. Receiving healing for any wounds in this area is crucial. Failure to do so can lead us to use ministry to prop up our sense of identity or self-worth and this distorts what the Spirit wants to do and also makes it unbearably painful if there is ever a disappointment or a failure.

How can we be used by the Spirit of God if we retain an implanted "caution button" about the Spirit put there by a false spiritual tradition, a damaging experience, or by our own lack of emotional openness? The disciples did wild and crazy things by anyone's definition. They were not at all cautious, hesitant, balanced, sensible, untrusting, unbelieving or closed off.

When people are regularly seeking to be empowered by the Spirit you can always tell because spiritual things often seem to happen around them.

If we desire to grow in ministry, we must grow in obedience, dwell in the love of our Father and increase our experience of the Spirit – and deal with the obstacles we bring to the party.

In so far as you do these things and seek to pray for people, I promise that you will see a measure of Jesus' ministry, without having to pretend to be perfect.

You can sue me if that doesn't happen.

Bad news for all perfectionists: it's OK for us to accept that there will always be a gap between our aspirations and our capacity. Imagine I get tickets to watch the parallel bars at the next Olympics and feel inspired to give it a go. I would soon discover the discrepancy between my aspirations and my capacity. Years of training go into what happens at the Olympics. It is unseen, but real and vital. So it is with ministry in the power of the Spirit. Anyone you know who God uses to do any of this stuff has established some of the spiritual foundations for ministry.

It is about us, who we really are, all of the time. Thankfully though, it's also about our God of grace, who he really is, all of the time too.

True story

"I had a very vivid dream in which I was run over by a red London bus and died. I thought I really had been and woke up in a cold sweat. I sat bolt upright and sensed that someone was asking me, 'What are you doing with your life?' I had no answer. My previous experience of Christianity was a heady combination of boring school chapel and guilt-inducing evangelical camps. But I decided to give Christianity one more shot. A friend recommended St Mary's. The first time I went I said to God, 'I'm not even sure I believe in you and I'm definitely not getting involved' – which now feels quite ironic, since I am ordained and lead a church.

As soon as I walked through the door I cried and experienced a sense of coming home. I carried on coming to Sundays and after a few weeks, found myself at the front, coming forward for prayer for first time. I didn't think the worship was very good that night, I had no idea what the talk was about, and am not entirely sure how I made it to front. I had, though, a very powerful experience whilst being prayed for that included feelings of electricity and struggle. When I finally 'came round' I was certain that God was real and powerful. The Alpha Course provided the intellectual grounding I needed and helped me make sense of what had happened. I had on-going experiences after that which were less dramatic and more about a sense of deep forgiveness and the love of God, my Father.

Here are some of the things I have seen God do.

Someone in my Alpha group nearly went home after the first prayer session on the weekend away. He hadn't experienced anything when we prayed for him and he was angry. I asked him to give it one more go the next day and to put the pressure on Holy Spirit and not himself. As soon as ministry started he went to front and hit the floor. He stayed there for hours. I asked him what had happened: he told me he had said to God, 'Give me one good reason why I should worship you.' The following Wednesday he told me that when he got back home that night, he found that his porn collection now repulsed him. He got rid of it there and then. He also tried to play the usual violent PlayStation game he loved, which involved shooting monsters, but realised that he didn't want to shoot anyone any more!

Another man I met had only come to one of the course sessions, but was desperate, so came to the weekend away. He worked for MTV, had cocaine and booze problems, and was sleeping with prostitutes. He had just been caught drink-driving for the umpteenth time and was being deported as result. He had no belief or church experience at all. Again, he experienced nothing during the first prayer session. During the second session though, he started screaming, growling like a lion and writhing around on the floor. Several people were needed to restrain him as we prayed for him. His life completely changed after this. He became a Christian, sorted his lifestyle out, moved back to his home country and started working for a church.

I was asked to lead a team to a church in Belgium. There was a woman I noticed during a time of prayer who stayed at the back of the room. I didn't know who she was. I felt God show me that she was holding pain in her stomach. I told her this and she didn't reply. I thought this must be purely emotional pain and prayed for her. It turned out that she had breast cancer in both breasts that had spread to her neck, to her spinal column and to her pancreas. The prognosis was very bad.

She was actually the leaders' wife and got in touch to say that the following week she had had a test. Her tumour count had dropped to 25, which is within the normal range of a healthy person. The cancer in her spine, neck and pancreas was completely gone, but the doctors couldn't believe it so they sent her for another scan and indeed, the second scan confirmed that all the cancer had gone.

The cancer that had spread to her second breast was gone and the primary cancer that had started in her other breast, which doctors said would certainly lead to a mastectomy, was so reduced that they didn't need to do anything other than a bit of localised surgery to remove what was now a very small lump. It was done in one day.

I would like to point out that I wasn't even praying for the right thing and that lots and lots of other people had been praying for her for a very long time. But this is still very encouraging to me and her doctors agreed it was an extraordinary recovery."

9
Paul's Letter to the Corinthians

In the next two chapters, we are going to consider the gifts of the Holy Spirit. In order to grasp how Paul thinks the gifts are meant to function amongst us, we need to understand what was happening in the church in Corinth. References here to the use of spiritual gifts in a worship context have inspired some to seek to exercise such gifts today. Perceived abuses here have been used to justify caution about, or non-use of, spiritual gifts today.

Let's have a little think about that before we go any further.

- This letter provides clear evidence of the Holy Spirit powerfully at work amongst people who were not a) Jesus himself or b) the apostles. The Corinthian experience of the Spirit is not unique in the early church, but it is does provide a rare glimpse of what worship was like then and how the gifts were used then.

- Paul begins his letter with a commendation of that church's openness to the power of the Spirit (1 Corinthians 1:4-7), in particular thanking God that they *"do not lack any spiritual gift"* – this despite some appalling mistakes the apostle feels compelled to correct in his letter.

- He does not tell the Corinthians to avoid spiritual gifts. On the contrary, he urges them not to be "ignorant" about them (12:1) and to actively "seek" them (14:1).

- He says they can all prophesy (14:31) and that he would like them all to speak in tongues (14:5). If we were to rule out aspects of church life because they might be abused or because there is a potential for misuse, we should consider banning the following:

- **Preaching.** If you have been in church for any length of time, you will have had to endure weak, wholly inaccurate, quasi-heretical and powerless speaking.
- **Worship.** Membership of a church will also have exposed you to terrible singing, instrument playing, inept and quasi-heretical song-writing.
- **Love.** If you have any experience of Christians then you will be aware of how rude, aggressive, selfish, competitive, undermining and jealous we can all be.

So the idea that we should minimise or neglect a spiritual activity just because "it could go wrong" would leave us with very little to do.

Leaving aside those who entertain interesting theological ideas about the cessation of the gifts after the apostolic era, I think others find the idea of exercising these gifts rather threatening.

We would have to take a risk to see them in operation and we wouldn't be in control if we did.

Of course, by contrast, we feel safe with such things as preaching, worship and love – on the illusory basis that we are actually in control of those things!

Naturally, it is hard to admit that we feel this way.

Context

I am indebted for this reconstruction of what was happening in the Corinthian church to Gordon Fee who wrote a brilliant commentary on 1 Corinthians and also an analysis of all passages mentioning the Spirit in Paul's letters in, *God's Empowering Presence*. These are simply the best books I have read on the subject of the work of the Spirit. He argues that the basic issue over which Paul and the church were divided was the question *What does it mean to be spiritual?* Some in Corinth largely associated being spiritual with speaking in tongues, the language of angels. They took this gift to be the sure evidence that they had already entered into the pneumatic existence of the future. For this reason, they had a great desire to use it when they met together.

Paul's letter is actually a response to a communication from Corinth. In their letter, they obviously not only defended their use of tongues, but also called into question Paul spirituality. Paul responds by defending his apostolic ministry (4:1-7), rebuking them for their arrogance (4:8-21), and also discusses his own use of the gift of tongues (14:18).

For the Corinthians, "spirituality" had somehow become divorced from the life we live in our bodies and so it didn't matter to them...

- ...if a church couple were living in an incestuous relationship (5:1).
- if church members were suing each other (6:1).
- if women wore a head covering in church (11:10).
- if the poor didn't get any food when they met to share fellowship (11:22).

Paul's correction of their beliefs about and practice of the gifts (chapters 12-14) will take up the rest of this chapter.

We need to know about the gifts of the Spirit (12:1)

The Corinthians couldn't afford to be ignorant about the gifts and neither can we. On the contrary, Paul insists that we should be proactive in seeking to know about spiritual gifts. Why?

Spiritual gifts are the "power tools" all Christians need to get our particular job done.

Our particular job is to advance the Kingdom of God, which Jesus did by the use of various spiritual gifts – preaching, prophesying, healing and delivering. When I first moved into a flat, I discovered that my drill didn't work on the walls. Brick walls need a hammer drill and I didn't have one. No amount of wishing the drill bit would work made any difference and neither did trying to force it to work.

- My good wishes don't make people better. Spirit-empowered healing does.
- My arguments don't convert people. Spirit-empowered words and deeds do.
- My good intentions don't change situations. But Spirit-empowered action like the laying on of hands and Spirit-directed prayer does.

The gifts of the Spirit are essential to the fulfilment of our calling as Christians, therefore we cannot remain ignorant about them. We need to know about the gifts in theory and in practice.

Shouldn't we seek more of the fruit of the Spirit (Galatians 5:22-23)?

No, we should not! We are to concentrate equally on both fruit and gifts, becoming more like Jesus in our character and in the ministry he entrusts to us – and get on with doing so.

We need to know about Spirit inspiration (2-3)

Just as all religions do not lead to God, so all expressions of spiritual power do not derive from God. The essential test is, does this spiritual activity point to the Lordship of Jesus? The spirit realm is not a neutral place in which all spirit inspiration is good inspiration – contrary to the relativism of our culture. Jesus is the Lord of the spirit realm and therefore, any gift we exercise must derive from him and point to him, or it stands in opposition to him. It follows from this that we should turn from those experiences of spiritual power or inspiration that do not point to Jesus and that we should not return to them having come to faith. Every gift we may have exercised in the past must now be surrendered (together with our whole selves) to Jesus, so that all we are (including our gifts) points to and glorifies him. Some people seek to do good with

102

their particular gift and others evil. But our moral intention is never the ultimate criterion with God. It is our response to the Lordship of Jesus that counts. Without an acknowledgement of him in all things, we are essentially living for ourselves and apart from him.

There are lots of spiritual gifts (4-11)

Paul's main point is obvious: the same Spirit inspires different people in different ways. So he rejects out of hand a boring uniformity (in Corinth, an over-emphasis on tongues) in favour of the expression of a rich diversity of gifts. He then gives one of several lists of possible manifestations of the Spirit in this letter (7-10).

In (12-14) Paul focuses on what should happen when the church comes together to worship.

He thinks of the Spirit as being like a dancing hand of inspiration who could touch anyone in the church and use them to express gifts of knowledge, healing etc., when they meet together. Paul uses different words to describe these things: "gifts", "manifestations", "works of power" – suggesting the whole picture he paints is suggestive and ad hoc. He could have highlighted other gifts, but these are the ones that came to his mind as he writes.

We don't actually know what all these gifts are and I think the best we can do is reason back from widespread experience to give definition to such things.

- *Message of knowledge* – the communication of information about a person or situation not known by the person communicating (12:8)
- *Message of wisdom* – the communication of what to do in response to a prophetic revelation (12:8)
- *Faith* – a supernatural confidence that God is going to do something right now (12:9)
- *Healings* – gifts that bring healing to us as we are in body, mind and spirit (12:9)

- *Miraculous powers* – probably refers to deliverance from evil spirits (12:10)
- *Prophecy* – the ability to communicate what God is saying now (12:10)
- *Distinguishing spirits* – the ability to discern whether what has been said or done is inspired by the human spirit, a demonic spirit or the Holy Spirit (12:10)
- *Tongues* – our spirit praying in conjunction with the Holy Spirit to help us express sighs and groans too deep for words (12:10)
- *Interpretation* – making known what a publicly given tongue means (12:10)

The Spirit inspires all of the above and manifests himself through us as he wants to (12:11).

The church is like a body (12-26)

Paul then develops the image of the church being like a body. There are many parts of a body, but they are all important to the right functioning of the body.

Although there are many spiritual gifts, they are all important to the right functioning of the church.

After all they derive from the same source (12:4-5,13) and are merely different expressions of the same body (12:12,14). So the real challenge of church life is to hold together a large number of people with a very diverse range of gifts.

And it is a challenge.

- If all the gifts come from the same gracious Giver, surely we shouldn't use our gifts as a way of competing with each other? But we do.
- If the gifts are merely different expressions of our own body, then we shouldn't despise gifts we don't have or don't understand. But we do.

- It is a mistake to think we can live without certain gifts (12:21). But we do
- It is a mistake to think that because we don't have certain gifts, we don't really belong (12:15). But we do.
- It is a mistake to despise the part we play on the grounds that it is hidden or "unimportant" (12:22-24). But we do.
- It is a mistake to write either ourselves or other people out of the script. But we do.

Diversity of expression sounds like freedom, but there are risks inherent in freedom – that's why many churches avoid it. The process of holding uniquely gifted people together can lead to pain and tension.

Let me offer you the coward's ways out.

It is to find yet another church in the hope that this one won't let us down (the quest for the perfect church) or to stop trying altogether.

The body has a kind of functional structure (27-31)

God has given us variously gifted people to help us regulate the life of the body. Paul describes particular people as gifts to the church (12:28f). Notice the lowly position of the speaker in tongues (28). In the functioning of a multifaceted body, we inevitably need spiritual leadership and guidance and perhaps especially people who understand the various manifestations of the Spirit to help us grow in theory and practice.

Gifts must be exercised in a loving way (13:1-7)

My brother suffered from mental health issues throughout his life. He had to see a psychiatrist once and in the course of the interview, at which several were present, the psychiatrist said to him, "If you think I've got any interest in seeing you get better, you've got another think coming – I don't care if you get better or not." Now,

I imagine he was trying to emphasise that my brother needed to take responsibility for getting better, but the way it was expressed caused him to leave the addictions unit he really needed to be in. Here was a gift of healing, but not one exercised in love.

It is absolutely essential that we exercise our gifts in a loving way – otherwise we might as well not bother.

I feel great sympathy for those who have had off-putting experiences at the hands of foolish or unloving Christians in the name of ministry like...

- ...being pushing over when they are being "prayed for"
- having pressure put on them to speak in tongues
- being emotionally manipulated by "prophecy"
- having stupid things said to them like, "You must have un-confessed sin in your life" or "you lack faith."
- being condemned when in need of grace

Our gifts are rendered spiritually valueless if we do not exercise them in a loving way – a point Paul makes as he lurches uncharacteristically into the quasi-poetic, often ill-chosen, marriage favourite of 1 Corinthians chapter 13.

I have no idea why anyone would choose this as a reading for their marriage.

It's like trying to improve your confidence in your appearance by going clothes shopping with a model. Or improve your tennis by playing with a Wimbledon champion. The only person who lives up to this characterisation of love is Jesus. Try taking the word "love" out of (4-7) and substituting your own name.

That probably didn't go well.

However, we are called to love if we want to exercise the gifts of the Spirit.

Prophecy vs tongues (chapter 14)

So Paul has just hyperboled that love is the be all and end all; it is the in all and through all, if you claim to be a spiritual person. It is love that is the true test of our spirituality, not how much we can speak in tongues. However, we aren't supposed to choose between being loving and exercising spiritual gifts – though I note that some loving people seem to find the concept that they are gifted difficult to receive, whilst some very gifted people struggle with arrogance and a lack of love. The reticent need to read on – we are told to literally salivate after the gifts; the presumptuous need to go back to 1 Corinthians 13, read it, and learn how to put it into practice.

We are now entering into a long compare and contrast between the value of speaking in tongues and prophecy. Imagine a church meeting in which everyone is speaking in tongues all the time – *that was Corinth.*

This led outsiders, or maybe new converts, to think they were super-crazy, because they couldn't understand what was going on. This also breaches Paul's definition of love, which extends to those outside the church and includes what is best for them.

Paul's response (14:2) is that speaking in tongues is addressed to God (and therefore is humanly incomprehensible). It's the sighs and groans too deep for words that the Spirit inspires in our spirit when we seek to articulate deep, deep things within ourselves that don't need precise formulation – like when we are extremely happy or sad or burdened in prayer. By contrast (3), prophecy has an impact outside of ourselves. It strengthens, encourages and comforts other people. Which means that a good question to ask about public prophecy is: *does it do what it's supposed to do on the tin?* If it doesn't, it's either...

- ...wrong
- more you than God
- shouldn't be publicly given.

Again, think prophecy (and any other gift) and immediately think love (something that helps other people) as your next thought. Therefore (4), whilst tongues fulfils the important role of strengthening or edifying our inner being as we express profound joys or burdens in the Spirit, prophecy can actually help other people. Everyone can receive the gift of tongues. In the Greek the text reads, "I want *every one of you* to speak in tongues, but I want *even more* that *every one of you* should prophecy" (5). This isn't a vain wish. If only that were possible (sigh). He wants *every one of us* to do this, including...

- ...those who have tried but haven't done it.
- have done it but didn't think the sounds they made were "from God".
- and those who are waiting for God to "God" them i.e. do something a bit more supernatural, so they know *it's really from God.*

Everyone needs a way of expressing themselves to God without the constraints of formal language. In everyone's life there are experiences that are too deep to be processed by rational formulation. Through tongues, we release ourselves and draw near to God and this process strengthens the bonds of love between us.

Speaking in tongues is therefore crucial for everyone. As Bieber rightly says, "You should go and love yourself."

However, Paul goes on, in a church meeting, if you all are rabbiting away in tongues all the time without interpretation (making your tongues comprehensible) then I say to you that prophecy is more important any day of the week, because it is already comprehensible and has the capacity to help other people and that is the whole aim of the game.

Just as everyone could do with speaking in tongues for themselves, we could all do with prophesying for the sake of everybody else.

Let me explain Paul's particular fixation with the gift of prophecy. What was the contrast between the gods of the surrounding nations and the God of Israel, according to the Old Testament prophets?

The God of Israel was a speaking God.

He spoke to his people through particular prophets and it was a national calamity when the voice of the Lord was rarely heard in Israel (1 Samuel 3:1).

So the sign that God is with his church isn't speaking in tongues. It is obviously a sign that the Spirit dwells within a believer and this gift is regularly received when people first come to faith – as it is in Acts where we read that they *"spoke in tongues and praised God"* e.g. Acts 10:46. The sign that God is with his church when we come together to worship, however, is that the voice of God is heard.

One difference now.

We don't have to wait for an Old Testament style prophet to show up. We are all able to discern what God is saying at a particular time and we are all able to prophecy. Not that everybody prophesying all the time would make for a good service any more than everyone speaking in tongues. But it is an important indicator that God is with us – not just to those on the inside, but also to those on the outside.

So (6) there's not a lot of common good in speaking in tongues by contrast with various forms of prophetic revelation or teaching. A tune isn't going to be discernible if the music isn't clear and no one's going to rush off into battle unless the trumpet can be clearly heard (8). So it is with us. Speaking in tongues is unclear in this sense. Without intelligibility we are just wasting air (9). What's the point in gabbling on in a language that is foreign to the hearer (10)? We should go for the gold of loving service when we meet together, as opposed to just strengthening ourselves – as necessary as that is (12). So no rabbiting away in tongues without an interpreter or without interpreting yourself.

Tongues is an expression of our praise or prayer (what we are saying to God) whilst prophecy is an expression of what we believe God is saying to the church or to someone. So the interpretation of tongues will be in the former category – it won't be a prophetic word. However, of course these are often given at the same time in a charismatic meeting.

Hence the confusion.

Once again (14-15), both of these gifts are of value. It's good to pray internally and intuitively in the Spirit and it is good to pray and prophecy rationally with the mind. The Spirit fills the entirety of our being to help and inspire us. It's just that the common good dictates that we need to be able to understand what is being communicated when we are together and therefore prophecy is of greater public value. We don't want to alienate outsiders (16) and we don't want to deliver a stonking prayer only to find that no one is any the wiser and can't even agree with it (17).

Paul then makes quite a boast:

He thanks God that he goes for it in tongues in private more than the tongues-crazy Corinthians. But in a public context, he'd always go for comprehensibility (18-19).

What do we take away from this?

Love, love, love

Not exercising a gift in love is a disaster, but the Kingdom is only advanced as we use the gifts we have been given.

As the old adage goes, "the answer to incorrect use is not disuse but correct use".

If you have suffered through the misuse of a gift, get prayer and receive healing and then get straight back on the gift horse.

And don't look it in the mouth.

Anything offered to God and anointed by the Spirit can be used by him. What does it mean to *"earnestly desire the gifts of the Spirit"* (14:1)? Well, what does it mean to earnestly desire food? Imagine you haven't eaten and you are in a queue for food. You are seriously hungry; all you can smell is that food, all you can think about is what food you are going to eat. That's the focus and desire we are meant to bring to being used by God.

Speak in tongues

Everyone can and no one has to. It's not the sign of conversion, you aren't second rate if you don't, but the opportunity is there for everyone to do it. Some find themselves doing it, others hear about it and do it. If a group of us were to put this book down now and all have a go at speaking or singing in tongues together would that contradict what Paul is saying?

Firstly, it is a mistake to think that Paul is promulgating new laws when he writes. He is responding to actual situations which need tailored responses, from which we deduce general principles.

Like, it's a mistake for the whole church to drone away in tongues all the time when we come together. That doesn't mean we can't speak in tongues to ourselves during a service or sing in tongues together for a comparatively short time. That at least has the effect of drawing us together into something and it often leads to the expression of other gifts. We just don't want it going on throughout the meeting and we must explain for the sake of outsiders when it happens.

Seek the gift of prophecy

This is another way of saying *get better at discerning what God is saying to you*. The whole point is that we have the Spirit living within us now and he wants to guide us. Bearing in mind that our subjective sense of God's guidance doesn't take precedence over the teaching of the Bible, our calling is to follow the voice of God in our lives, as Jesus did. Sometimes, he shows us something that is for someone else.

Prophecy isn't teaching – that's a premeditated reflection on the Scripture. Prophecy is unpremeditated and contributes to the question *What is God saying in this very moment to some people or to one person here?* Teaching should apply to everyone whilst prophecy is more particular. That's why a word can really leave you cold whilst it really speaks to your friend. It could be a feeling or a knowing, it could be a word or phrase or an image in your mind; it could be a specific passage from the Bible; sometimes it's enacted through a gesture or dance.

Anyone can play, but you should first ask, is this for me?

- If it's definitely for you, I wouldn't give it. People can be so surprised/pleased that God has shown them something that they feel they have to share it because "It may be for others too."
- How can you tell if it's God? You can't. Just give it and if people respond, it was. If they don't, normally no one will know. Think of yourself as a spiritual post office worker. Your job is to deliver the mail not check the contents and see how people respond to it.
- Do you need to describe the imagery by which the word comes? Maybe sometimes, but in general, probably not: "I see a picture of a Walrus with lovely white fur and a pine (or is it a conifer of some kind?) and a river that is three quarters full. I believe the Lord is reminding us that he made the world." This could simply be given as, "God is reminding us that he made everything".

Go for maturity (14:20)

This is easily written, but represents one of the great challenges of the Christian life.

Stop thinking in a child-like way.

Children believe inaccurate things and behave in immature ways – and so they should. At some point though, we cease to be children and are called to grow up into maturity. Leaving behind childish ways includes believing what is real about life, ourselves and God; it means aiming to live as though I am actually a Christian and not some strange hybrid, and it means valuing the calling and gifting God has given me.

Here, it means taking something pretty basic on board.Paul essentially says (21), "In the Old Testament when God speaks to people and they don't understand, it's not a good thing." The way in which the Corinthians are speaking in tongues all the time is making that gift act *as a sign for unbelievers.* Doesn't Mark say, *"These are the signs that shall follow **the believers**: they shall speak in tongues"* (Mark 16:17)? Doesn't Peter realise the Gentiles have received the Spirit because they speak in tongues, just as he had on the Day of Pentecost (Acts 10:46)? How then can speaking in tongues be *a sign for unbelievers*? Surely it is a sign for believers – a sign that they have received the Spirit?

It is – don't worry.

But in a situation where everyone is speaking in tongues and the unlearned, ignorant or unbelieving are present and cannot understand what is being said, if they dismiss it, tongues can act *as a sign against them*. God sent foreigners to speak to his people but they couldn't understand and didn't listen, says Paul (14:21), quoting Isaiah 28:11-12.

The fact that they couldn't understand doesn't mean God wasn't speaking though.

In the same way, if someone concludes that something spiritual, like speaking in tongues, is mere gibberish they come to the wrong conclusion about something spiritual *and draw God's judgement upon themselves.* The Corinthians were allowing that to happen by their indiscriminate use of the gift. Paul argues that our aim is to bring God's salvation to outsiders, not his judgement.

Just to confuse things further, Paul goes on to say that prophecy is *a sign for believers* (22). Has he not just argued that because prophecy is comprehensible, it can benefit outsiders in a way that speaking in tongues can't?

Yes, he has – don't worry.

Prophecy is a sign for *unbelievers*. But primarily, prophecy is a sign to *believers* that God is with them and we can tell he is with us most of all by the impact of what he does in the lives of unbelievers when we come together to worship.

There speaketh the evangelist.

We don't want scenario 1 – an outsider can't understand what is going on (23); we want scenario 2 – they can (24).

I believe that the implication here is that when we come together to worship in the Spirit, with love for one another, seeking the gifts of the Spirit and lifting up the name of Jesus, the power of the Spirit is released. He moves over the people who are present. He convicts this one of sin, he reassures this one of son or daughter-ship, he fills that one, he anoints that one for service and in these he releases the expression of various gifts. And round the edges, just looking in tentatively from the outside are unbelievers or those who don't understand; and to these he wants to reveal Jesus through signs and wonders, including revelation, accurate words of knowledge and prophecy that goes to the heart of who they are (25).

How many times have such people started to cry during services in our church; how many times have they courageously gone up for prayer at the end? I remember having a word about the forgiveness of sins and a woman became a Christian by coming forward weeping and collapsing into my arms in front of everyone.

This is what we want to see when we meet together.

I spoke to a woman who was just passing by the church and noticed that people weren't wearing formal clothes. This was different from her experience. She came to one service and couldn't stop crying. However, she wasn't sure she would be welcome in the church and so didn't come back for a while. Some months later, after she had just started to try and process the pain of her troubled past, she had a dream in which she heard a voice telling her to go back to the church. She attended once and was moved again and then came to one week of the Life Course, during which she told us her very painful story. We felt compelled to pray for her and she experienced God's love for the first time and spoke in tongues.

On the same occasion, a young guy who had attended church for three weeks, having been invited by a friend, also let us pray for him. He cried and felt a rush of power pass through him. He also became a Christian. It was their experiences of the Spirit in our services that made both of these people open to God and what he might be able to do for them.

What can we do to see this happen more?

- "Everyone" come ready for action (26). I think our pre-match prayer meeting helps with this. Sometimes the manifestation of the Spirit is greater there than in the service. Anyone can play when they are inspired by the Spirit as long as they keep their eyes fixed on the main qualification, which is love or "the strengthening of the church".
- We need to regulate the flow of gifts and to do so isn't to grieve the Spirit (27).
- We see that public tongues requires interpretation – for all the reasons previously explained. Charismatics regularly confuse the interpretation of tongues with prophecy, but in fact they are different gifts. It's because these gifts naturally happen at the same point in our meetings. At the moment when one person feels moved to give a public tongue, someone else may feel moved to give a prophetic word. If someone gives a public tongue and you have a prophecy, wait for a bit to see if there is an interpretation of the tongue before giving your word from God.

Thanks to all those who have found the courage to go for the expression of the gifts in a public context; you set a great example.

But if you find yourself doing this a few times consecutively, step back and see if others will play, because to do this is to prefer other people. If you know you really should say something but you just aren't sure, go for it because that is faith. There is no absolute certainty in this area. We don't know it is God, but we believe it may be. Err on the side of courage not caution, as long as you do what you do in love.

It's better to think; "It probably is God, bearing in mind that it might not be" – as opposed to, "It probably isn't God, bearing in mind that it could be."

Paul argues for a tongues and interpretation burst followed by a prophetic burst (27/29). Notice that we can all prophecy (31) and that prophetic people are fully in charge of themselves when the expression of their gifts is going on (32). So there's no place for "but I have to give my word *now*" or "I need to give my word for 10 minutes." The Spirit doesn't possess us; he wants us to co-operate with him as he prompts us to exercise our gifts. There is a place for the regulation of what happens in a service (33).

Does this include women (33b-35)?
I believe this is a rare example of an interpolation in the New Testament – that's to say an insertion by a later scribe who is copying the Greek text and expressing his own understanding of what should happen in church.

- I notice first of all that this instruction appears to have been pasted into the flow of the argument and stands out like a sore thumb.
- Secondly, that the author references the law in a way that Paul never would as an authority and that his teaching on women elsewhere (especially in Ephesians where husband and wife are radically told to be subject to one another) is far more nuanced than this. I just cannot believe Paul would ever say "It's a disgraceful thing for a woman to speak in church."

- Also, what are we supposed to make of (11:5) which envisages women praying and prophesying in church or of his affirmation of Priscilla who clearly led a church with her husband (though she is always mentioned first) e.g. (Acts 18:2-3)?

So writing as a non-woman, I recommend that you ignore these verses entirely.

Be teachable (36-38)

Paul then rebukes the arrogance of some in Corinth who have developed a superiority complex, effectively saying, "Look, I'm the apostle round here and you aren't and I've been playing the game longer; in fact, I initiated you into the game in the first place." Sometimes, people have become Christians at St Mary's and have then gone on to develop different ideas, especially about the Spirit, inspired by other teachers from elsewhere.

This isn't a problem in itself.

It's not like I have a monopoly on ideas about the Spirit and some people from elsewhere are used far more powerfully than I ever will be and we should all seek to learn from them. There's only a problem when a comparatively new Christian starts to exhibit an assumed position of superiority. I can't help thinking, "So, not very long ago you weren't even a Christian, but five minutes later you now know far more, and are more open to the Spirit than me, and won't hear anything I have to say?"

It's not a question of right or wrong, it's a question of humility.

I advise us to always show respect for those who brought us to faith and for older Christians in general. The horrible truth is they usually know more than we do. It is at least worth thinking about the advice they give. You may decide to go a different way – that is your prerogative – but at least show them you have heard what they say.

Let's really go for the expression of the gifts

Let's go for it on the prophetic front (39a) – though not at the expense of speaking in tongues (39b). There just has to be a proper understanding of the role and value of each gift and some regulation of how they are expressed in a service.

Conclusion

This is what I think Paul means when he says *"everything should be done in a fitting and orderly way"* (40). Sometimes this verse is used against us when the Spirit moves in power and people are obviously touched or crying out in a distressing way etc. What Paul means is...

- "EVERYTHING i.e. all the gifts I have mentioned should be DONE in a decent and orderly way."
- He does not mean, "NOTHING WEIRD OR SUPERNATURAL should be done around here."
- Nor does he mean, "NOTHING THAT IS NOT CEREBRAL OR UNDER OUR CONTROL should be allowed to happen."
- And he certainly doesn't mean, "NOTHING that isn't IN THE LITURGY should be allowed to happen."
- The "order" we are looking for in our services is not the order of the graveyard, where everything is done in a fitting and orderly way because nothing happens – apart from a little grass trimming and whitening of the grave stones. He means, "Go for the order of the nursery, where anything could happen and the room needs to be brought back to a place of order somehow before someone gets hurt."

Let's go for that. It's much more fun.

True story

"I was going through a season of severe depression and suicidal thoughts. I worked from home and during the afternoons, life would tend to get a bit too much, so I would get into bed to sleep for a few hours.

On more than one occasion, normally through tears as I fell asleep, I would pray, "I do not want to wake up, in Jesus' name." I wanted to die, but was scared that God would send me to hell. So I wanted him to do it and save me the job.

Thankfully, God didn't answer these prayers.

Over the course of my life I had received several prophetic words from people about coming into a "wide open space". I would visualise a beautiful field full of lush green grass, the sun shining and rivers running, blue skies and other lovely features. Though I could see the field, I felt I could never walk into it.

I was in church one day and felt the Spirit was at work in me as I listened to the preaching. I went forward for prayer and a friend said he had a picture of a glass wall being smashed. Then another friend came over and gave me exactly the same picture. I didn't know what it meant, but it obviously meant something. Around a month or so later, some people were praying for me. I had mentioned my depression and suicidal thoughts and at the end of the session, a lady laid a hand on my head and said, "Depression go in Jesus' name." Instantly, I felt something like a heavy blanket lifting off of my body. I was instantly set free from depression and suicidal thoughts.

The next time I pictured the field, I was walking into it. It was like the glass wall that had been holding me back was no more."

10
Paul's Letter to the Ephesians

The concept of "church" is so beautiful. All kinds of people coming together under the same Lord to establish his Kingdom upon the earth.

The theory of the church is breathtaking.

There is just one little problem, just one small fly in the ointment, one tiny cloud on the horizon, and it is *the people who make up the church.* The people are like an *ugly great gash,* ruining what would otherwise be a perfect canvas. I've been a church leader for decades now and so when I say "the people" I really mean *you,* the people who make up the congregation.

A fellow leader once told me he had received a warning that a member of his church was planning to *storm the stage* whilst he was speaking. There would have to be a good reason why someone would want to do that, right? Want to know what it was? A member of his staff team had cancelled an evangelistic supper.

You people are so difficult.

Always complaining, being needy and not doing what we leaders ask you to do. All leaders quickly discover how many members of their church feel "called to rest" at any given time. Have you heard of the so-called "military year off" in the first year of marriage? Some extend that into a decade and others choose to take that time off even though they've never been married. After a while, you come to love the people who show up. This always makes me think of one of my spiritual heroines, Kate Gray, who stands by the internal doors in my church and opens them during services so they don't squeak and distract people.

How many are like her? Not many of you.

The people of the church are such a problem and, of course,
So are the leaders of the church.

All leaders behave atrociously and, of course, I am no different – unless "worse" is different. The same leader who told me about the stage-storming incident also told me about a time when he was preaching and there was a crying baby that just wouldn't stop. He looked at the mother and at his team but they did nothing about it. So finally, he got out an imaginary gun and pretended to shoot the baby. Then he had to make a public apology and this incident slowed down the growth of his new church plant for quite some time.

The leaders of the church are such a problem.

They are demanding, over-sensitive, controlling, weak and fail to practice what they preach.

We are all problem people, aren't we?

We sing about the perfection of God and all his ways and then behave as though we've never actually heard of him at all. We get in the way of what God is doing and yet, paradoxically, we are the people God loves to use and, astonishingly, we continue to be his only plan for the redemption of the world.

Seriously, why?

Best guess? This is to the glory of God who *"takes the weak and foolish things of the world to shame the strong and wise"* (1 Corinthians 1:27) and that's why it's not a compliment to be called a Christian. We are God's sick joke, told against those in the world who really think they have got it all together.

In this chapter, I want to talk about the two great polarities of the church, its unity and diversity, drawing upon Paul's letter to the Ephesians. This will help us, I hope, to identify what kind of "Spirit person" we are and also how to value and relate to the other "Spirit people" in our church.

The Unity Of The Church

Christian unity is not...

- ...everyone thinking and doing the same thing
- agreeing with everything the church leader says
- refusing to challenge our brothers and sisters
- denying that we've been hurt because these feelings aren't very Christian
- failing to do what we think God wants us to do because someone else in the church wouldn't like it.

Christian unity is our common belief in the one true God and our common submission to his holy, loving ways in the power of the Spirit.

In Ephesians (1-3), Paul explains what God is doing in history. As John Stott observes in his masterful commentary, "Through Jesus Christ crucified and raised from the dead, God is creating something entirely new. Not only is there new life for individuals, but also a new society is coming into existence. Not only is an alienated humanity being reconciled, but also a new humanity is being created. It is a huge vision. And at this point in the letter, Paul moves from an explanation of what God has done to what we must do, from mind-bending theology to the down to earth implications for everyday life."

Here's his argument (4:1-6). He appeals to them as *"a prisoner of the Lord"* (both a prisoner of Christ and for Christ), as an apostolic leader who has authority to tell them how to walk the talk because he is doing so himself. He urges them to live as though they believe what they believe, focusing first on the qualities we need to make relationships work.

He says, *"Show these kinds of qualities in your life together – lowliness, meekness, patience, tolerance and love".*

It doesn't take much to see that if we consistently did this any problems of disunity would considerably diminish.

Why should we bother?

Paul tells us to do all that we can to maintain unity (4:3). As Stott says, "The **one** Father creates **one** family, the **one** Son creates the **one** faith, hope and baptism and the **one** Spirit creates the **one** body. We are to maintain 'the unity of the Spirit' because we imitate God. Just as we are to be holy because God is holy and love because God is love, so we do what we can to maintain our unity as a body because God is **one**."

Yes, but how?

You may already have leapt ahead to the "how" question. We all know we should be unified. We also know that there are horrendous examples of disunity within and between churches and we ourselves may have suffered as a result.

So the real question of church unity is, how do we do it?

First things first: we are not being asked to be completely humble and gentle etc., *on our own*. We do not have what it takes to pull this off, though we often seem to behave as though it's all up to us.

So, as with all things Christian, the first place to start is with the Holy Spirit.

The qualities of character mentioned are actually "fruits of the Spirit" – expressions of his power at work in our lives. So when we are finding it difficult to hold things together with other people, the Holy Spirit should be our first port of call. This is something to remember all the time as we fulfil Paul's command to *"go on being filled with the Spirit"* (Ephesians 5:18).

Paul instructs us to *maintain* our unity, which must mean that it is possible *not to*.

Let's consider some common "unity destroyers":

- *pride* (a determination that my way is the best and only way)
- *aggression* (I am going to get my way by force if necessary)

- *impatience* (why can't you see that my way is the best and only way?)
- *disregarding one another* (because you don't see things as I do, you have no value)

These qualities make up *a perfect disunity cocktail,* our drink of choice when we revert to type, behaving with a defensiveness that suggests we think it's up to us to look after ourselves. Being a Christian doesn't take away personality flaws, personality clashes or strong disagreements. It shows us how to behave when they happen. So how do we maintain unity? Let's give these a try:

- *humility:* give no time to proving how spiritual you are and never jostle for position or recognition in the church.
- *meekness:* restrain your natural, immediate response to a situation.
- *patience:* in a dispute, try to understand where the other person is coming from.
- *be longsuffering:* give people a good chance to change before you open your great big mouth.
- *love:* make sure you are doing what you can to promote the genuine welfare of your church community.

Paul's uninteresting mystery (3:6)

So this is the mystery revealed by God to Paul that energised his mission and got him into so much danger: *"the mystery is that through the Gospel the Gentiles are heirs together with Israel, members of one body and sharers together in the promises in Jesus Christ."*

How interesting is it?

Surely, the answer on the face of it is "not very" for the vast majority of us. We haven't come from a background like Paul's in which those who were Jewish by birth considered themselves to

124

be marked out by God as against the rest of the Gentile world and separated from it. For Paul, it was a monumental change to come to believe that membership of the people of God now had nothing to do with "works of the law" (like being circumcised) but simply had to do with faith in the new thing God had done in Jesus.

Paul explains that two dividing walls of hostility separate humanity (2:14f): the first dividing us from God because of our sin and the second dividing Jews from Gentiles because of a wrong understanding of what it meant to be the people of God. Paul always insisted that in Christ, and through his death on the cross, these walls of division have been destroyed. So the coming into being of the church has huge implications. It offers the hope of peace. Personal peace as we are reconciled to God and communal peace as we accept others who have also been reconciled on the same undeserving basis as ourselves. There is an expectation resting on us to show the world how people can resolve issues of strife within our community of peace.

Oh dear.

But this does make Paul's mystery more interesting. It follows from this that the answer is never just "Jesus", it is also "the church of Jesus" – whatever the question.

- We are not free to disregard the church.
- Christians have to belong to a church.
- And, no, "church" isn't meeting with your two best buds in a mutual appreciation society.
- Believing in Jesus is not enough.
- Mere attendance is not enough.
- You need to be personally engaged with the people that make up your church and with what your church is trying to do.
- Otherwise, when do you ever need to display humility, gentleness, patience or love?
- Anyway, unity isn't about your preferences!

It's about what God wants to do *in us* and *through us* despite everything that may be true *of us*. So enjoy a depth of relationship that will require you to display the Christian virtues Paul mentions and find appropriate ways to get involved.

Disunity really matters. Have you been let down by or hurt by someone in church?

Here is my advice:

- Pray first and pray for a while. Don't leap into trying to sort it out.
- If it can't be resolved through prayer alone, have the courage to talk about what happened in a humble, loving way.
- Is there another way of seeing what has happened?
- Be ready to apologise for anything you can apologise for.
- Don't be a doormat, just "leaving it with the Lord" and depriving someone of the opportunity to change – even if they can't take it now.

Conversely, be ready to respond properly to criticism. All of us have blots on the landscape of our lives and those who see us in action get to know them. You should be aware of your negative press – what everyone who knows you would say about you when you aren't there.

Here's an idea: if people make the same or similar criticisms of you repeatedly, humility says, "They're probably right."

From the perspective of heaven, the church's unity is indestructible, just as God himself is indestructible. But that doesn't mean we can simply tut and dismiss the disaster of disunity. That isn't compatible with "being eager" to maintain the unity of the Spirit. I eagerly want Arsenal to win every match they play. Eagerness isn't really compatible with "it's not that important" or "c'est la vie".

Jesus created a community out a of rag-tag group of

incompatibles. The early church followed this pattern. Indeed, *"all who believed were together and had all things in common"* (Acts 2:44). It wasn't just the inspired preaching of the apostles or the signs and wonders, it was also the attraction of a shared life of love that caused the early church to grow so rapidly. In so far as we can create united communities of love, there is always hope. This is why we should do what we can to set aside irritations (as opposed to outrages) or annoyances (as opposed to irreconcilable differences). If we can give that a go, maybe people will look at our relationships of love and want to know what our God is like.

It is a tremendous challenge.

But love is universally appealing and in what is often a loveless world, a community of love stands out – and is a powerful argument in favour of the Gospel we proclaim.

This is what makes maintaining unity important.

Diversity (4:7-16)

Paul cannot think about the unity of the church without immediately discussing its diversity. Consider Paul's list of gifted people here and ask who you identify with most.

This expresses the one original thought I have ever had and so it is very important – to me.

Some people find this helpful, some people hate it. I don't mind; you go your way and I'll go God's! Paul says that these variously gifted people are to do their thing and that this will promote the maturity of the body by building it up in its multifaceted ministry (Ephesians 4:11-14).

We can't put people in a box, and we are obviously complex beasts, but I believe that there are three main drives that we tend to express as people in different measures.

- An outward focused drive that puts us more in the apostolic or evangelistic camp. Adventurers (as I call them) value risk-taking, impact-making, stimulation, freedom, passion and they love projects and tasks. They are entrepreneurial and tend to exist in a group, if you can ever get them to join one, by leading it.

- There is an inward focused drive that puts us more in the pastoral camp. Carers value such things as love, relationship, community, friendship and trust and they love long-term people continuity. They are highly relational and tend to be good at making sure people in a group feel supported. They will definitely be in a group(s).

- Then there is the nebulous third of any trinity – a drive which has regard to the way we do what we do or why we do what we do, which puts people more in the prophetic or teacher camp. Truth-tellers value such things as integrity, honesty, justice, process. In a group, they are good at process questions and critiquing what we do. They will be in a group until they leave it because it is no longer being true to what it ought to be.

They are all necessary to the group.

In my opinion, adventurers ideally lead because they want to initiate movement. Carers are anti-movement and Truth-tellers don't really swing into action until something is moving, even if they can see what should happen. Adventurers, who are concerned with fulfilling tasks and projects, should aim to have a Carer on one leg asking, "What about the people?" and a Truth-teller on the other leg asking, "What about the principle?" They should, however, lead and not be held hostage by their Carers or Truth-tellers. Ideally, all three should respect and trust each other.

Paul's idea is that churches need all of these drives working together so that the people in any given church might grow up into maturity. This happens as we see what more mature versions of ourselves look like in action and also as we interact with and learn from those whose drives are different from our own.

In my view, all churches are meant to benefit from the ministries of all these gifted people. In so far as they don't, the church is always poorer for it. What tends to happen though is that leaders of churches collapse their vision into what they are good at and fail to release the breadth that is really necessary for true church health to be promoted.

- Adventurers create adventurer playgrounds which are all about the mission of the church and the people who go are little more than fodder for the further expansion of the church.
- Carers create small, warm clubs that don't really have a mission beyond looking after the people who are "in".
- Truth-tellers create either prophetic playgrounds which are too pure to be appealing to outsiders or preaching halls that are too cold to belong to except at a cerebral level.

There is no underestimating how different these drives are. Let's see how the Adventurers, Carers and Truth-tellers get on when it comes to going to the cinema.

A group of us have decided to go to the cinema and the fact that a group have decided to do anything means absolutely nothing to the Adventurers. They will go to the cinema if they decide they will find the experience of going, the people going, or the film itself stimulating. Carers on the other hand will absolutely have to go with the group, even if there's a flood and they hate the film. Truth-tellers on the third hand, will primarily be motivated by the question, "Is going to see this film the right thing to do?" They will want to discuss this question for longer than it has already been discussed.

- Adventurers have too strong a sense of identity apart from other people. They are too aware of the distinction between themselves and the rest of the world.
- Carers have trouble defining their identity, finding it hard to

distinguish themselves from the rest of the world.

- Truth-tellers believe they see themselves in every identity, that in fact they are part of the whole world!
- Adventurers only think they can do particular things very well.
- Carers don't think they can do anything very well.
- Truth-tellers think they can do everything well.
- Adventurers are pragmatists.
- Carers are people-people.
- Truth-tellers are principle people.
- Adventurers are too focused and struggle with narcissism.
- Carers aren't focused enough and struggle with co-dependency.
- Truth-tellers leave things too open and struggle with arrogance and inertia.
- Adventurers get things done.
- Carers get to be with people.
- Truth-tellers like to process and theorise.

Some of us are more like kings or queens, some more like priests and some more like prophets. We all need a king or queen to lead us, but every ruler needs to reminded of the principles on which he or she rules and of the true needs of the people over which he or she rules.

So who are you? Usually people identify with two drives.

The true dilemmas of church unity are often unconsciously fought out between these diversely gifted personality types:

- e.g. should we follow the leader's flash of vision or should we engage in a proper process of reflection first?
- e.g. should we give more focus to the mission of the church, the needs of the people in the church or the correct doctrine and right behaviour of the church?
- e.g. if we are going to welcome outsiders, we may need to tolerate un-Christian behaviour or lifestyle choices; where do

we draw the lines?

- e.g. if we are going to focus on what would help believers grow, how are we going to guard against creating something that only we can understand? To what extent do we have to explain everything? Do we have to restrain our openness to the Spirit in any way?
- e.g. does the church exist for the benefit of its non-members, is the church a family or is the church a prophetic challenge to injustice?

If you instinctively want to say, "It's all important," I would agree with you. But to hold these things in tension and to define the balances between them is the real challenge of church leadership. The potential for disunity lies in our struggle to get this right, given the fallen nature of everyone involved, ourselves included. We tend to believe that our personality and preferences are the true barometer of what God wants – even though we know that can't really be true. The trouble is, that's what everyone else believes too.

This is exactly why we desperately need the Holy Spirit.

True story

"When I was 3 years old, my parents divorced and what followed was a very messy custody battle for me. My dad was an alcoholic who would tell me that I was worth nothing and unlovable. I would go to church with my mum each week, but I never felt I belonged there. Every other child would attend with their mum and dad, while I would sit in the pew hearing that God was an amazing Father. But for me, a father was a negative figure and I didn't want another one in my life.

Over time, unable to relate to God as my Father, I became frustrated and others things in life became much more attractive to me than church. Eventually, I walked away altogether. When I was 18, I reached out to my dad in the hope of restoring our relationship.

I told him that I wanted to get to know him, but that he wouldn't be able to drink on the day that we met up. He responded by telling me that alcohol would always come first. I walked away from the relationship and this was the last time I saw him.

Following this, feeling lost and very much alone, I moved to London and got into a long-term, unhealthy, controlling relationship. I worked in fashion and did everything I could to forget what had happened. I became completely defined by my role at work and by being successful. When I look back, I can see that I was trying to prove to my dad that he was wrong about me.

One day, out of the blue, a friend asked if I would like to go to church with her. As I walked through the doors, I felt I had come home. As I opened myself up to the Spirit, I began to receive healing for what had happened in the past. As I allowed God in, childhood dreams of working for a church came back to me and before long I changed my job and started working for St Mary's.

Since then I have seen the Spirit move in me and in others, and in particular how he uses the painful and broken bits of our lives for good when we are filled with the Spirit.

At one stage, I was asking God for fresh vision for my work. I was standing with my eyes closed and hands open, inviting the Spirit to meet me. I was overwhelmed with compassion for the local community. I felt myself double over as the Spirit of God refilled me. I knew God was doing something deep within me. I believe God showed me something of how he feels about people in our local area, how he would use me to make connections with these people and how this was not to be done in my own strength. The sense of God's compassion remains with me now. I am seeing more and more people in our community respond to the outreach work we do with children and parents. I find that as I have become more open to him myself, he has done more through me.

In our Kids Church, there is a child with autism who often feels angry at the world. On one occasion, I watched as the Spirit fell on him during a time of prayer. His eyelids started to flutter, his hands started to shake, and his facial expression changed. Another child walked over, placed a hand on his shoulder and simply prayed, "Thank you, Jesus." It was obvious that this young child was being filled with the Spirit and that a deep peace was resting on him. Afterwards, I asked him how he felt and he told me that all the busyness of his mind was still and that he now knew that he could ask Jesus to be with him and bring peace.

We all prayed for another child to be healed when he broke his thumb and he got better to the great surprise of his parents and his class. I have seen God do many things like this."

11
Preaching

I would like to restate the proposition that *the Holy Spirit is the person in whose dimension of life we experience God*. Therefore, without the inspiration of the Spirit, there can be no true preaching. In fact, it doesn't matter whether the task before us is preaching or visiting a sick friend, without the inspiration of the Spirit our impact will be limited to what we ourselves are capable of. And this may be quite considerable; we can be clever, kind and insightful. But this isn't the same as being led by the Spirit, bearing fruit and glorifying God by the use of our spiritual gifts, as we are called to do.

I do not mean to denigrate the spiritual experience we may have gained over the years or the professional skills we may have acquired. I am simply drawing attention to the fact that preaching begins with our current experience of Jesus.

Communing with Jesus today is the only starting place.

This alone helps me to know what God wants me to speak about (if it is up to me), what God wants me to emphasis from a particular passage (if it is a given) and crucially as well, this helps me answer the question, "What does the Holy Spirit want to do *after* I have spoken?"

Preaching is about us, everything that we are, on a day to day basis. Therefore, an authentic experience of preaching in the power of the Spirit begins long before we speak.

- Since we shall never be without sin, we have to come to Jesus to be cleansed every day.
- Since our identity is always being challenged, we have to come to the Father to be reminded of who we are every day.
- Since we grieve and quench the Spirit and simply run dry quite easily, we have to come to Jesus to be filled with the Spirit every day.

An unprocessed heart produces confused preaching. Knowing how to make the heart still in the presence of God is the indispensable preparation for true preaching. We have to come to God all the time to be reminded that he is still the Lord over all things, despite what may be happening in our life or in other circumstances.

Coming to God as he really is and as we really are makes preaching in the power of the Spirit possible.

I pray with my wife first thing in the morning and then for an hour before doing anything else – most days. I was once invited to give a series of sermons at a liberal Episcopal church in the States and have never seen a more shocked reaction to the Gospel. Here were sincere people who had grown up in church and wouldn't countenance not going, but who lacked any idea of what Jesus had done for them. One morning after I had been praying for five minutes or so, I had a day-dream in which I saw many people come to the front after I had preached about the cross. I found the scene in my imagination very moving and then it dawned on me that God wanted me to make such an appeal that night. I was confident no one would ever have done such a thing in this extremely white, bright and polite church.

After I had spoken I invited any who wanted to come forward to give their lives to Jesus to do so. Many did and this was an unprecedented event in the church's life. I was invited back a few more times over the years and reckon that maybe 500 people were impacted by the Spirit over this time. But I think the critical moment of breakthrough was when I responded to that prompting of the Spirit to invite people to come forward that night. The preaching of the Gospel was, of course, crucial, but my point is that following what you believe the Spirit wants you to do afterwards is equally crucial and this I discovered in prayer beforehand.

I have noticed that conservative evangelicals often find preaching to be a source of stress and concern. Presumably, this derives from their understanding that the Spirit only really works through the correct exposition of the word.

This does put a lot of pressure on the preacher!

After all, according to this view, preaching is the only means by which people can be pastored, hear from God and remain in the truth. By contrast, when I come to church I expect to meet the Spirit in the worship, to hear the prophetic word of God at some point and to see him at work in the ministry time afterwards. These connection points are *in addition* to hearing the word of God through preaching, which the Spirit also uses.

I don't find speaking burdensome; in fact, I really enjoy it.

Eric Liddell famously refused to run on a Sunday and yet won gold in the 400 metres in the Olympics of 1924. He rejected the lure of missionary work despite huge pressure from his family, in favour of running. He said, "When I run, I feel his pleasure." I totally relate to this. When I speak, I feel his pleasure. Whether anyone else does is a moot point.

- I enjoy the confidence that comes from believing God has inspired what I have to say.
- I enjoy making people laugh.
- I enjoy being myself when I am speaking.
- I enjoy shocking people who do not go to church by what I say.
- I enjoy discovering what I actually think. I am an external processor and so have been genuinely surprised by some of what has come out of my own mouth.
- I enjoy what God does afterwards to confirm the truth of what has been preached.

Practicalities

When we preach we should aim to be *barbeque man or woman.* Hopefully, everyone knows what it's like to be at a barbeque amongst friends, with a glass of wine in our hand, on a hot summer's day, talking in a relaxed way about something we feel passionate about. On these occasions, we fully inhabit our own speaking.

When we preach, we shouldn't want to be anyone else, saying anything else to anyone else.

In order for us to be truly ourselves, exposing our actual thoughts and feelings about the subject we are dealing with, we have to begin with God. By God's grace, we have the capacity to be securely connected to our Father and filled with his Spirit. When our preaching comes out of this experience, it matters less what others think about us. There is no unattainable standard to pass and no terrible fear of inadequacy. Do you know why people say they often remember a story that was in a sermon more than the teaching content of the sermon?

It's because the story was properly communicated.

Speakers more fully inhabit the stories they tell, especially when they come out of their actual experience. In other words, stories in your typical sermon function as rare moments of authentic communication. The trick is to make the whole sermon like this.

A good preacher is a bad preacher that got better. There are very few "naturals". Most people have to learn how to preach. We have to learn to be comfortable expressing what we think in front of people. We have to learn how to master the technical side of communication – using a microphone, a stand and, increasingly, an iPad for images and verses etc. We have to learn how to make sense of a biblical text, even if we have a background in theology. Also, we have to learn how to be inspired by the Spirt as we speak, so that we can clearly communicate the sense of what we believe he is saying.

To remain open to the Spirit is a challenge.

With experience, we can always knock something adequate together or rely on someone else's thoughts or go back to something we have done before and regurgitate it. I'm not saying that strengthening our content through the wisdom of others or reflecting on our last thoughts about a subject is wrong. I am just making the same point repeatedly: that our first port of call should not be ourselves and what we bring to the party. *Our first port of call is God.*

A theology of church meetings

I don't believe Paul expected much that happens in worship to be premeditated. Undeniably, most good preaching is premeditated, *but this makes it unusual.* The classic charismatic reputation for poor preaching is well-deserved, in my opinion. While conservative evangelicals over-emphasise the role of preaching, charismatics don't emphasis it enough. Just because we rely on the immediate inspiration of the Spirit for gifts, like prophecy or words of knowledge, doesn't mean we have to do that for preaching. I once heard an astonishingly interesting sermon based on the list of people who rebuilt the walls of Jerusalem in the book of Nehemiah. I say "astonishing" because when I heard he was speaking from this passage (Nehemiah 3), I thought, "This will be incredibly dull." After he'd been speaking for half an hour and doing a great job, he suddenly announced that the Spirit was leading him in a different direction. What followed was dull and confused and I left once we passed the hour mark.

Being led by the Spirit can happen prior to a meeting without us letting God down and with preaching it normally does.

Preaching, like everything else in the service, should be subject to the question, "What is the Holy Spirit saying or doing on this particular occasion?" Sometimes people have given prophetic words earlier in a service that have effectively summarised what I feel I should be preaching about. This is always incredibly encouraging. This makes me confident about what God is saying or doing on that occasion and when I am confident of that I am dangerous – in a good way.

I remind us that prophecy is a more important gift than teaching according to Paul, and that these gifts are not the same thing. Neither are they mutually exclusive, of course. Paul values prophecy above all because of the potential evangelistic impact on unbelievers when facts about them are made known; when *"the secrets of their hearts are laid bare"* (1 Corinthians 14:25). Unbelievers are meant to conclude that this must be God and go on to put their faith in him. As an evangelist above all things, Paul thinks of Christian meetings primarily as evangelistic contexts. Teaching believers comes second and so does speaking in tongues, something that unbelievers cannot understand.

Because I am only human, despite my best efforts to turn up ready to preach as a man of the Spirit, either my brokenness or inability to process what may be happening in my life sometimes gets the better of me. This doesn't stop God using me, but it will potentially limit the effectiveness of my preaching. However, when I am in a worship context, acknowledging my emptiness before God and being ministered to by God, I might at the last minute become aware of what God really wants me to say, having struggled with that question up until that point. I might at that moment receive from God what I actually need to say rather than what I feel I should say. God can make us ready during the service if we weren't ready before. But normally, I think we should do what we can to come ready for action.

Being realistic, anyone who has experience of preaching knows there are some sermons that are effectively "set pieces" – we know what we want before we start. In my own context, that would be huge Christmas or baptism services, which we regard as "guest services". If we have gift days, we know what we are hoping will happen!

That doesn't mean it's OK not to connect with God, just because we already know what we want to say. One of the stories included in this book is about a word of knowledge I had that someone present at a gift day was thinking about what to do with £10K. A couple had been setting aside money for a while and had accumulated that amount of money. This shows that God is even at work when church leaders speak about money and their generous giving certainly helped the gift day. I also give pretty much identical evangelist talks on the Life Course, but I believe that prayer releases the power of the Spirit to bring new life through the same talk on a particular occasion.

How do we know what the Spirit wants us to say? Obviously, if we are speaking from a passage in the Bible, we should explain what it means, since this given content has already been inspired by the Spirit. We should also make sure that the passage does mean what we think it means by using a good commentary. But the way we communicate it, and the particular applications we make in our context at the time we are speaking, should also be inspired by the Spirit. When we are preparing and praying, we may sense that the Spirit is drawing attention to something in particular. Over time, we learn to recognise his direction when we are praying about our preaching.

What is the Spirit doing after the preaching?

This is the final challenge of preaching: to discern how the people who hear you are meant to respond to what you have said. I stress this because in order to be true to the model of Jesus, we always have to be concerned with word and works. Sometimes, Jesus taught and then did miracles and sometimes he did miracles and then taught. Preaching which excludes an opportunity for response underestimates the impact of Spirit-empowered communication. It doesn't do enough to help people who could be changed by the Spirit immediately in response to the word of God.

The question *What does the Spirit want to do after we have spoken?* may be readily answered by the passage we have used or the plan we have been asked to fulfil e.g. this is a guest service. And I believe that occasionally the Spirit wants people to understand what a particular passage is saying. But normally, the Spirit wants to break into people's lives so that they can be healed or comforted or renewed in strength in response to the word of God.

This is why, with the exception of formal occasions when there are lots of guests around, we always pray for people after our services. I believe that the speaker is the most natural person to lead us into ministry because, hopefully, God's power has been resting on that person as they have spoken. So, prior to preaching, we need the kind of worship that can lead us into the presence of God and the kind of service leadership that is open to what the Spirit might want to say or do before the teaching happens. We also need a trained ministry team to pray for people afterwards, so that the power of Spirit-inspired preaching is not diminished in its potential impact.

If teaching was enough, Jesus would simply have taught. It wasn't then and it isn't now.

So Spirit-empowered preaching is about all of us, all of the time. It is the product of our own on-going communion with God that helps us to offer to others the wisdom, inspiration and hope we ourselves are living in. It requires a humble acceptance that teaching is only one of the things the Spirit might use to reach his people when we come together and that our communication must be sensitive to the particular context the Spirit is creating on that occasion. Finally, it must lead to the transformation of lives – not merely to the conviction that what has been said is true or inspirational, but to the opportunity to experience more of the power of the Spirit who is right here. He doesn't merely convict or inspire us. He is also present to transform us into the image of Jesus, so that we can actually do what we might feel convicted or inspired to do. We all need regular opportunities to open ourselves to the person of the Spirit for his healing or empowerment in response to inspired preaching (amongst other things) when we come together as believers.

I am not sure what else church could be for.

Evangelistic preaching

Recently I wrote a book about this subject entitled *Message: Send – communicating the Gospel in a post-truth world*. Space prohibits me from going further into this subject here.

True story

"I grew up in a Christian family and can't pinpoint a 'Damascus road' moment in my life. Rather my story is about coming to know the reality of God's love and power for myself. My parents always loved me – however, I wasn't sure they always loved themselves and I picked this up. I doubted my own worth in a massive way. For instance, when I had just started secondary school, I was in town with a group of friends and we went into a shop to look at a new video game. They all ran off and hid leaving me alone inside, as a joke. I had a very strong reaction to this experience; I felt incredibly alone and spiralled into feeling completely unloved and worthless.

However, I remember pacing up and down the garden and realised that if God was real, he was all I needed. Suddenly I felt an immense assurance that I was known and unconditionally loved by God. It came from nowhere, from outside me. In those few moments, God told me I was going to study at Oxford and meet my wife there, which I subsequently did.

As I grew up I went to Soul Survivor every summer. When I praised God, I would encounter him in the same way I did in my garden and I felt the same love wash over me. But although I saw the Holy Spirit do amazing things, I was never really involved and assumed this was only for really special men and women of God.

The churches I attended did nothing to counter the view that the Holy Spirit was just for the spiritual elite and I had no understanding of how he could work in my day-to-day life. My encounters with him became more like a series of one-night stands and not an ongoing relationship. And so rather than relying on God to help with my issues of worth on a consistent basis, I learnt to 'self-soothe' through performance. I discovered I could sure myself up through academic and sporting success and through relationships with the opposite sex. If I could demonstrate to others I was top of the class, played for all the sports teams and was desirable to the opposite sex, perhaps I could convince myself that I was loveable as well. I gradually let go of God's unconditional love for me and became a caricature of myself. No matter how much other people might be impressed by my 'success', I was unable to receive anything from it, knowing it was the caricature that they loved.

I am sad that this carried on for such a long time. The impression I gained from church was that I had to earn Jesus' love, through trying to be a nice. Jesus became a kind of go-to person if things were really bad, but I was generally taken up with my own religious performance.

Coming to St Mary's was a bit of a shock! Firstly, because I immediately encountered the Jesus I had met at the age of 11. But that wasn't all: a number of ORDINARY people spoke detailed prophetic words into my life. For instance, I work in finance and in 2016, I more than doubled the amount of revenue I made in 2015 – which doesn't matter, except that someone from St Mary's, who I had never met before, told me in November 2015 that this was going to happen. It didn't shock me that God would speak to me, but it did shock me that he'd use ORDINARY people to do it! I was sure there was some secret trick somewhere. Perhaps when I wasn't looking, these apparently ordinary people were secretly memorising whole books of the Bible, or foregoing sleep to worship and pray all night?

Here are a couples of stories of God at work in my life.

Over a number of years, my wife and I had saved £10k – maybe with a view to starting a charity one day. I went to church on a gift day praying, 'God, if you want us to give this away, make it clear.' The speaker said he believed there was someone in the congregation who was in two minds about whether to give £10k or not. His words hit me between the eyes. I was shocked that God would speak so directly – but that was nothing compared to how shocked my wife was when I told her what I had prayed before the service. After much soul searching, we gave the £10k away. Amazingly, the very next day at work we were effectively given the exact amount back.

We took the youth group from our previous church to Soul Survivor. One morning, the talk referenced receiving the gift of tongues and a few of our group stood up in response. As their leaders, we were asked to pray for them. After a little while, I noticed that one of the boys was responding. So I moved closer to him and prayed more specifically that he would start speaking in tongues. I knew there was power in the room because when I prayed in tongues, I unexpectedly became aware of a new fluency and richness to my own prayer language. But rather than speaking in tongues, the boy started to wretch as if he was about to be sick. We continued to pray for him, but that only seemed to make the shaking and retching worse. Eventually, it got so violent that the boy started screaming and fell to the floor, where he began to writhe around.

At this point, I felt out of my depth. I thought you just invited people to speak in tongues and they did. Then all of a sudden, the boy became still on the floor, opened his eyes and stared at me. But these were not his eyes; they were so big and vacuous. The boy would later tell me that he was trying to speak to me, but something was preventing him. The boy closed his eyes again and then became as still as a corpse. Honestly, he looked like he had died. I thought, *'Well, there's the end of my promising ministry career.'* I prepared my explanation for the Soul Survivor authorities: *'It's all St Mary's fault; they taught me everything I know.'*

But then, fortunately, he came around. He opened his eyes and I could see the 16 year-old I knew again. He asked me, 'What just happened? I don't remember anything.' We prayed a final time for him and encouraged him to try and speak in tongues. Then suddenly, this beautiful language erupted out of his mouth."

12
Healing

Learning From Jesus (Luke 5:12-16)

Let us recap: Jesus taught about the Kingdom of God and demonstrated its nature through signs of wonders. The role of the disciples wasn't to stand back and lead the applause when yet another sick person got better as Jesus touched them, it was to learn how Jesus did what he did and then go and do it themselves. So there is a reason Luke places this healing story after Jesus' prophetic pronouncement: *"from now on you will be fishers of men"*:

This is what he means by "fishing for men".

It won't be long before Jesus sends the disciples ahead of him to heal and cast out demons (Luke 10:17-20).

Despite much evangelical huffing and puffing, there isn't a biblical basis for the view that miracles ceased after the ministries of Jesus and the apostles. Certainly, as Paul says, *"where there are prophesies they will cease and where there are tongues they will be stilled ... when perfection comes"* (1 Corinthians 13:8-12). But this perfection isn't the completion of the canon of Scripture but the Second Coming. It is only when Jesus returns that, *"I shall know fully, as I am fully known."*

Obviously.

On the contrary, the clear command of Jesus to teach future disciples to obey *everything* he commanded to the first batch is there for all to read (Matthew 28:18f). It would be as logical for me to argue that Jesus' command to love our neighbour no longer applies to disciples after the apostolic period. It makes no sense to me that we should seek to preach the word of the Kingdom, but have no expectation of performing the works of the Kingdom.

With all due respect, the fact that some churches may not do this stuff doesn't mean anything. Nor does the fact that you may not have seen anyone healed yourself. What about churches that do and people who have? In any case, spiritual reality isn't defined by our experience, but by what we read in the Bible. For this reason, if you are a Christian and you have never seen a sick person healed, I wouldn't stop bothering God until you have.

"If God can use some Christians to heal, then why not me?" is a good question to ask God.

Of course, anyone who considers the historical record without disallowing the evidence can see that, again and again, Christians have healed the sick in the name of Jesus.

Why should you miss out on all the fun?

So that's enough human limitation, false doctrine and unbelief. What do we learn about healing from this passage?

1) Sickness is bad (6)

There are many awful diseases, aren't there? In fact, yours doesn't even need to be a terrible disease to negatively impact your life. Now, I say *sickness is bad* because you never find Jesus leaving sicknesses unattended because a) he thinks people deserve them b) because they are being taught an important spiritual lesson through them, or c) because they are being punished by God with them. Yet that is precisely how some Christians wrongly "explain" some sicknesses.

Why do Christians want to believe things like this?

Partly because they get the impression from the Old Testament that the sovereign God is the author of good and evil (such as Isaiah 45:7). *In the Old Testament.*

However, in the New Testament there is a recognition that God is not the only player on the stage of human affairs. We play a real role and so does our enemy, Satan. This is a good instance of what happens if we take the Old and New Testaments to be co-equally valid sources of information about God. In fact, these beliefs, though popular in the church, cannot be reconciled with the New Testament. Sickness is no more or less that a symptom of the diseased human condition commonly known as sin. Not your sin personally, most of the time, but just the sinful context in which we live out our lives. It is a manifestation of the brokenness that Jesus is against. The salvation he brings isn't just for the soul: it is a holistic well-being that begins when we receive Jesus and will be completed when we see him face to face, when he comes again – this has an impact on everything about us, including our bodies.

It is always good to ask Jesus to take sickness away.

2) Jesus is willing to heal sickness (7)

Step one in seeking healing is not to want your sickness for any reason. You certainly don't want it to become your identity. Step two is to ask him to take it away. The centurion is utterly convinced that Jesus can do it: he doesn't even need to detour to his house to get the job done: *"Just say the word"* (8). He has a disease problem and he knows Jesus can sort it out. It doesn't matter that he's a Roman and Jesus is Jewish – it's like, problem/solution, let's not waste time here. Note that Jesus acknowledges the man's confidence and asks him no supplementary questions like:

- "Do you need to repent of anything?"
- "You know I'm the Saviour, right?
- "You will become one of my disciples after this, yeah?"

He just heals because this is in the job description he received from his Father. Remember that God chucks his grace about indiscriminately. Any sickness is potentially a healing waiting to happen.

3) The question of authority

The centurion, a military man, recognises Jesus' authority (9).

He probably sees the way in which Jesus gives commands to sicknesses and demons and they vamoose. This makes sense to him; he discerns that here is one who is "over" these things and they obey him.

It is very important that Christians believe that they too have been authorised to heal the sick.

Remember that there is a sense in which Jesus is the model for our attempts to heal and a sense in which he isn't. Jesus is like us in kind, but not in degree, as discussed earlier. The reason Jesus carried such spiritual authority is because he was perfectly obedient to his Father, perfectly received and gave out the love of his Father and was filled with the Spirit without limit. We shall always be a work-in-progress until he returns. This is why we need to pay attention to the unseen foundations of ministry and this is why our experience of healing will never be exactly the same as Jesus'. But even though many people we pray for will not receive all they want to receive, we shall still see amazing things if we sign up to be involved in the ministry of Jesus on a consistent basis.

4) Faith is important (10-11)

Jesus is astonished by the centurion's faith given that he is not a son of Abraham. Please note that neither faith nor authority have anything to do with *how* we pray:

- Shouting a lot, proclaiming that someone is healed or acting in other bizarre ways like clicking our fingers angrily carry no power whatsoever.
- In fact, could you try to be as normal as possible when you pray for healing?
- It is weird enough praying for healing, especially if you are praying for a non-Christian; why dial up the weirdness factor?

Faith is a simple thing and something that everyone is entirely familiar with. Who do you have faith in? People who have proved reliable. Why does this man believe that Jesus can heal? Because he's seen him do it again and again. Faith is confidence and confidence increases as faith is vindicated. So you can grow in faith and faith can increase in a room as things start to happen – or it can decrease. I have seen this happen on many Life Course weekends when we teach about the Spirit. As God starts to touch some people, the expectation of others rises and so more happens.

Occasionally, I have felt pretty confident that *this is going to work*. I once had a clear impression that God wanted to heal people with foot problems in a particular meeting. We even put out the precise number of chairs beforehand for people to sit in. The chairs were duly filled and all the people prayed for were healed – unusually in my experience. But more commonly, when people tell me they've been healed, I feel compelled to ask them, *"Are you sure?"*

This is because I believe – and I don't believe.

- Never tell someone they haven't been healed because of a lack of faith; this simply adds to their burden. It's bad enough being sick.
- If there is a problem with a lack of faith it will probably be yours as the person doing the praying.
- I have seen people who have tremendous faith die.
- I have seen people with no faith immediately healed.
- I have no explanation for this.
- Always be kind.

Pray that you will live to see things go into super-drive (14-16).

This is party time! And again, it is humbling and astonishing to be present when God acts like this. I don't think anyone can really predict when this kind of intensity will occur or why, but again, we can see that faith is raised by faith. I was very surprised by what happened at New Wine over one summer when my church was leading Venue 2, as it was called then. I would say it was the most powerful spiritual event I have ever been involved in leading. The factors I can identify include:

- Well-led worship.
- Good teaching.
- The power of people opening themselves to God over several sessions and several days.
- Personal desperation and faith amongst the people being prayed for.
- Many powerful testimonies.
- Increasing openness and increasing power in ministry.

I felt compelled to host a number of conferences called Third Person (from whence came the title of this book) to restate ministry in the power of the Spirit, because so much happened despite the fact that we were doing nothing different from what we would normally do on a Sunday in church. If this sort of spiritual intensity could happen sometimes through some churches, why not much more often through more churches, I thought?

What do we need to see healing happen (Mark 5:21-43)?

I think the answer to that is quite obvious from this passage. You need the conviction that Jesus can do it. From where do most people in this account get that conviction? From the fact that they were actually seeing him heal people.

It's not rocket science – like so much in Christianity.

He is now at the stage in his ministry where large crowds follow him wherever he goes (5:21). Presumably, in the hope or expectation of seeing healing, many people just left what they were doing and followed Jesus around. So this amounts to a temporary suspension of the necessary (working to stay alive) in order to witness the amazing. Jairus, the synagogue ruler, is willing to sacrifice his standing amongst the other religious leaders to get healing for his daughter (22-23). He ignores the necessary (the authority of his superiors) for the sake of his daughter. The woman with the flow of blood is willing to lay aside any concept of ritual purity in order to touch Jesus (25-29). She ignores the necessary social constraints governing what it meant to be a woman (and a sick one at that) to get what the doctors couldn't give her. So the conviction that Jesus could heal was so strong that it overcame everyday necessity, religious authority and social convention.

This powerful conviction was held by some – but not by all.

From a theological perspective, Mark's Gospel is an examination of the question, *What does it mean to have faith in Jesus?* There are plenty of people in the story who don't get it, even though they must also have witnessed healings:

- Many of the religious leaders of the day didn't get it (3:5)
- His family didn't get it, including his mother (3:21f)
- His disciples often didn't get it (4:13)
- Even those who were the beneficiaries of healing didn't always get it (5:15-17)

It is not self-evident that we will put our faith in Jesus – even if people tell us amazing things, or even if we see them with our own eyes.

In 2008, thousands of people flocked to Lakeland, Florida, in the hope of being healed or seeing healings. Thousands more watched the broadcasts every night. If Todd Bentley told the sick to get out of wheelchairs, or to receive healing by touching their TV screens, they were often healed. Some of the stuff you could watch on YouTube was weird – either theologically or in practice, or both. But during that time, anyone who wanted to see real healings happening in

Jesus' name could do so whenever they wanted. Sometimes you couldn't tell exactly what had happened; sometimes it was obvious that something spectacular had happened. In general, I was astonished that anyone couldn't see that it was God. But then I believed; there are many who adamantly didn't, despite what they were seeing and hearing.

Such is the challenge of faith.

- Are you worried you don't believe enough to receive healing?
- Are you worried you don't believe enough to pray for someone else?

Join the club.

- Having faith and not having faith is completely normal.
- Faith increasing and faith decreasing depending on what happens is completely normal.
- But ultimately, faith isn't the *feeling of faith* (as nice as it is to have that flowing through us), it is our obedient response to the command of God.
- I pray for people whether they are healed or not because I believe I am called to do so.
- Actual healing belongs to God and not to me.

I have been praying for people for about 30 years. When I hear great stories of healing or become aware that God is moving in power in a meeting, I can feel full of faith, ecstatic even. I often cry when this happens. Maybe it's a bit of compassion, but really crying has always been my particular response to the presence of the Spirit. I get particularly excited when I discover that some conditions have been healed that will never naturally clear up on their own. But then someone says something that undermines my confidence (often something quite legitimate) or I feel I've made a mistake in my leadership of a meeting, or not much happens and my feeling of faith diminishes. I never understand why more hasn't happened when I want it to. But healing remains mysterious, I think, and not something that we can fully contain within any framework.

When the Lakeland Revival was going on, Todd said he prayed for people for between four and twelve hours a day. And this unsustainable pattern of ministry exhausted him and probably contributed to a mistake he made in his personal life. I am not suggesting we seek to emulate this, but it does raise the question, *How much do we want to see healing happen?*

We want the body, don't we, but we don't want to go to the gym.

I go back to a point I made earlier, which is that God uses people who show up. I believe that this is God's perspective: he is delighted by any attempt we make to show faith. He is like a father watching a child struggling to learn a new skill. He doesn't expect us to do what we cannot yet do.

- To receive prayer is to express faith.
- To pray for someone is to express faith.
- Faith is the magic with God and he loves every expression of it.

When we experience a deficit in the faith department, let's come to God who has the resources. *"I believe, help my unbelief,"* says one man to Jesus (Mark 9:24).

True stories of physical healing (from June 2008 at St Mary's)

We held special meetings to pray for the sick at this time and I asked people who felt they had been healed to email me:

1. Someone fell over during a blackout and damaged a tooth. She also bit the side of her cheek and probably tore muscles/ligaments in her jaw as well. She couldn't open her mouth and was told by a

doctor that she would need to eat by using a straw for some time to come. After prayer, she was able to eat normally, to the surprise of a doctor friend.

2. A couple felt drawn to the church, wanting to explore issues of faith. He had been depressed for a while, but after prayer at the first service he attended felt much better in the week. So the next week he went up for prayer again for pain in his neck and shoulder. When prayed for he fell over and the pain went.

3. Someone had been wrongly diagnosed with depression when they actually had a hiatus hernia. After prayer, she was healed of the effects of the hernia and reduced the level of anti-depressants wrongly prescribed to the minimum level with a view to coming off altogether.

4. Someone who was healed some time ago of damage to the discs in his back went away from church and coincidentally came back for the first time when we started to have special meetings to pray for the sick. The back condition had returned but he was healed again after prayer.

5. Someone who had pain in both knees claimed they were significantly better after prayer.

6. Someone who had pain in their neck was healed after prayer in the pub after a meeting.

7. Someone who had been in hospital because of stomach pain found that the pain had completely gone after prayer.

8. Someone was healed of back pain during prayer then reconciled his relationship with his estranged father and started inviting his brothers to church.

9. Someone else found that both knees felt significantly better after prayer.

10. Someone was healed of Crones disease who went on to eat normally from then on without any ill-effects.

11. Someone responded to a word of knowledge concerning a broken left foot that had not mended properly. After prayer she

found that it was significantly better.

12. Someone had developed an ever-increasing range of food intolerances over twenty years. She was prayed for and felt she had been healed of most of these intolerances, having eaten things she couldn't previously eat without any reaction.

13. Someone, before prayer had three X-rays demonstrating the need for a bone graft into an injured hand. When doctors came to operate they could find nothing wrong – but put in a wire anyway, concluding they must have made some kind of mistake!

14. Someone with a form of incurable vertigo was prayed for at a distance by our staff team so that they could travel and get treatment after an attack. They found that for the first time there were no symptoms of the disease at all.

15. Someone who had pain in his hips spreading to his groin was prayed for before a long flight. Afterwards, there was no pain anywhere.

16. Someone was completely healed of Celiac's disease, a condition of the colon.

17. Someone was completely healed of nerve damage in their hand after an operation went wrong. He then had full feeling in his hand.

18. Someone had suffered from a life-long tremor in her body, but it appeared to have almost completely disappeared since she received prayer.

19. Someone with leg pain for 17 years was healed after prayer.

20. Someone who strained their shoulder dancing was healed after prayer.

21. Someone was healed of a life-long allergy to alcohol (*is that a good thing?*)

22. Someone was immediately healed in response to a word about a frozen shoulder that had been hurting for over 6 months.

23. Someone who responded to a word about constriction in the throat was healed that night.

24. We prayed at a distance for someone who was told by doctors that they might have to have their heart stopped and restarted. In answer to prayer this procedure was found to be unnecessary.

25. Someone was told that their extreme vertigo would probably continue even with medication for 6 weeks. They received prayer and although nothing happened immediately, the next day they were completely better.

26. There was someone who had had cystitis twice before and this could only be cured by antibiotics. The symptoms were happening for a third time when they were prayed for. She was immediately healed without any need for antibiotics.

27. Someone who found it difficult to shake off cold bugs and had refused prayer because nothing seemed to happen was prayed for at a distance during a meeting and was better the next day.

28. Someone with a sleep disorder for over a year and pain in their neck and shoulder was completely healed after a prayer meeting. They said, "I can now do all the things I have not been able to do for at least the last year."

29. Someone on antibiotics for a week was healed of mastitis after prayer.

30. "I hadn't been able to eat wheat or dairy products, or drink wine, tea or coffee for the last five years. I was standing for worship and I felt something strange happening in my body. I dismissed it at the time," one person said. She then decided to try eating a sandwich about a week later and found there was no problem. So she tried all the other things she couldn't eat and has been fine ever since. "It is a wonderful blessing to be healed. Praise the Lord."

31. Someone was healed of 12 years of painful periods after prayer. She was prayed for many times, but then on one occasion, "A great heat and a sense that he had healed me" came upon her. She stopped taking medication and has now been fine for months.

What's not to like?

Here is an account of one of the most dramatic healings we have seen in the history of our church.

True story

"A group of us met on a regular basis. We would pray for and encourage each other in whatever we were doing for God. As always happens with these kind of things, we got to know each other very well and became incredibly close. So you can imagine our sadness and shock when we found out that one of us had become very ill. This became a regular situation we prayed for. My friend had a heart condition that was worsening all the time.

Even though we prayed for healing (and she went to helpful hospital appointments and saw good doctors) it seemed that every week there was something new. A new level of the heart condition that was hurting her more and more. It came to a point where her housemates had to stay with her overnight when she went into hospital. She was now beginning to have mini heart attacks on a fairy regular basis. Although she was given medication to help control it, there seemed to be a continual deterioration of the condition. It got to the point where she was put on the waiting list for a heart transplant. She wasn't getting any better. We were praying and continuing to ask for healing and it wasn't happening.

But then one Sunday something crazy happened. We had a normal church service, but at the end of it, we were invited to give words of knowledge about what we thought God was going to do. There were various words and pictures given, but one stood out to me. Someone said they had tingling in their left arm and it could be something related to a heart condition. I can't explain it, but I had this sudden urgency to get my friend (by any means possible) to go to the front and receive prayer. We encouraged her to go to the front and all decided that we would pray together in response to this word.

I struggle to explain exactly what I felt. As I started to pray, my friend began to cry. She eventually fell to the floor and wept. A feeling of anger flowed through me. Looking back, I think of this as 'righteous anger'. I don't remember exactly what I prayed, but I don't think it really mattered. What I remember was how I felt and how desperately I wanted God to do something.

Eventually, we all stopped praying and my friend sat up. She said 'Guys, I think I've been healed.' I have to say that despite the experience I had just had, I was unsure how to respond to that. She had weekly check-ups at this point, so we encouraged her to go and see her doctor and see how it went.

We had a text the next day. She was better. The doctor was amazed and commented that he wasn't usually able to take anyone off a transplant list because they got better. She had been healed. It still doesn't really seem real. She is still fine today, years later. I cried as she told the story in church and watched as people's faces showed their absolute shock and amazement at what had happened."

13
Deliverance

The Lies of the Land

The transfiguration is a mind-blowing event (Mark 9:2-7): the super-bright clothing, the sudden gathering of Spiritual Hero Avengers from the Old Testament, the God cloud and his audible voice. This is a high point, an extraordinary respite, and a necessary moment of communion to strengthen Jesus for all that is to come.

It was balm to Jesus' soul even if it was terrifying for the disciples.

However, this mountain top time-out was soon to come to an end. In a painfully short time, he has to come back down again; back to face all the familiar obstacles to the fulfilment of his mission.

We are warned that just as the world treated Jesus, so it will treat us (John 15:18). This holds true for what happens in the spiritual realm as well, where we find that *"our battle is not against flesh and blood but against the hosts of wickedness in the heavenly places"* (Ephesians 6:12). A world in opposition to the ways of God and an antagonistic spiritual realm create an obstacle course for us as we seek to follow God, the nature of which I am going to expose so that we might be inspired again to confront and fight as Jesus did.

It is very common to find that a time of God's blessing is followed almost immediately by one of challenge. Sometimes they come at the same time. I mentioned leading Venue 2 at New Wine, where I saw some of the most powerful ministry in the Spirit I have ever seen. But it is not an exaggeration to say that I actually divided my time that week between travelling to and from a local garage and leading the meetings. Amazing power was released as the week progressed, but out of my car came all kinds of problems – four different and unrelated problems that plagued me with anxiety because I was due to drive through France the day after the conference.

So the car had to be OK.

And it was – on the very last day. My son also appeared to develop a very serious medical condition, just before I was due to speak. This also came to nothing. None of this prevented God from working, but it was a challenge for me. These attacks are, of course, a back-handed compliment. We are, at least temporarily, in the right place at the right time, doing what God wants us to do – and so we are opposed.

Of course, Jesus didn't have to wrestle with the potential cars have for demonic manipulation; he had to deal with even more serious things. I think it's worth drawing attention to all of these, because we are so used to them that we often cease to see them for what they are.

The brute stupidity of the people

A Gentile woman might be able to recognise Jesus' authority over evil – *"Yes Lord, but even the dogs under the table eat the crumbs"* (Mark 7:28) – but the people of God, who should be able to recognise their Messiah, rarely do. They veer wildly between greeting him with wonder (Mark 9:15) and potentially throwing him off a cliff (Luke 4:28). They go on to welcome him into the Holy City as they would a King, and then bay for his blood a few days later. I saw a spoof Bond play once which included a line I have always enjoyed:

"Let the girl go; she knows nothing. *She is really stupid.*"

The people are really spiritually stupid. Jesus repeatedly tells those he heals not to gather even more of a crowd. The crowd dynamic was obviously unhelpful to what he was trying to do much of the time. But they repeatedly ignore him and here we are again with a crowd and an argument – two of Jesus' favourites (Mark 9:14-29).

When we pray for people in the power of the Spirit, we regularly find ourselves having to deal with the effects of sheer human stupidity – either our own or someone else's. Some of the things we do to each other in parenting or marriage are staggeringly stupid, but often we are simply replicating patterns of behaviour we have experienced ourselves. People come forward seeking healing for the long-term effects of stupid treatment at the hands of parents, lovers and others. And as I have repeatedly made clear, we are also part of the problem. The damage caused by stupid behaviour is calculated to undermine our identity and render us ineffective in the service of the Lord.

It's not just the crowd though, is it...?

...It's their religious leaders in particular

The self-righteous, self-serving religious people, always ready to confront an act of astonishing mercy in the Gospels with a quibble about the rules. On a scale of 1-10, how spiritually arrogant do you have to be to worry about whether someone should be allowed to take up their mat and walk on the Sabbath *when they've just been healed*?

Did they not notice the healing bit?

How lacking in discernment and perception do you need to be *to demand a sign,* straight after the feeding of the 4000! (Mark 8:11). It's not like these guys and their crowd have this same spiritual power and authority flowing through them, so that any old Bobbins can do this kind of thing.

Jesus is doing unprecedented stuff!

Why not at least hold back from judgement, take a long-term view or even, Lord have mercy, hear what he has to say? He walks down the mountain right back to the religious – his least favourites. The teachers of the law are arguing (Mark 9:14).

It's what they do.

He effectively dismisses the lot of them, the crowd and its leaders as *"an unbelieving generation"* and wants to be done with them – *"how long shall I stay with you?"* (9:19)

Often, when we pray for people, we are helping them deal with the malign effects of religion e.g. the absence of any understanding of grace, the inability to receive forgiveness or to accept God as a loving Father. If people have reduced Christianity to a religion for you, then your religion will involve working for God's approval, being uncertain that you have it and seeing him more as a judge than a father. It will also be about being judgmental towards other Christians and towards those outside the church.

These attitudes are the opposite of what God desires and they offend him.

If we were only to read Jesus' invective against the religious in the Gospels (e.g. Matthew 23) we would not conclude that he was a very loving person. He comes over as a righteously angry person – though never towards those not pretending to have it all together. I was once asked to speak to three groups of students about the Holy Spirit in preparation for a mission and someone used their influence to make sure the invitation was withdrawn. Apparently, having me to speak about the Spirit would "create disunity".

That was a mistake.

"By what authority are you doing these things?" he wanted to know when we met to talk about it.

"Really? You want to ask me, with no sense of irony, the question the Pharisees asked Jesus?" I thought to myself.

The next day he became sick and that lasted for quite a while. My Bible reading for that day read, *"God will strike your enemies with sickness."* I doubt that Jesus was that bothered about my anger or disappointment. But he's not keen on anyone who actively gets in the way of the Spirit. If I had gone to that weekend, the Spirit would have empowered quite a lot of young people for evangelism. It's not something to oppose – especially if you call yourself a Christian.

Then there's the dullness of the disciples themselves

They will be God's solution going forward, but at this stage they are just as much part of the problem. Peter discerns that Jesus is the Christ (Mark 8:29), but then tries to prevent him from going to Jerusalem, eliciting the harshest rebuke (8:33). He and the others are like the blind man who when he is first prayed for, can see people walking around as though they are trees (8:24). The disciples see and they don't see.

Jesus believed his Father wanted him to go through Israel, preaching the message of the Kingdom (Matthew 9:35). This would serve as a prophetic revelation of his Messianic identity. But his main focus was on those he chose to be with him. The signs and wonders were performed in front of crowds of onlookers, but it was the disciples who were trained and commissioned to take up his ministry. The parables were taught to all and sundry, but it was the disciples who were are given the opportunity to ask questions and understand them (Mark 4:34). It is almost as if as soon as their leader Peter, gains *even the faintest glimmer* of understanding that he is *"the Christ"* (Mark 8:29), Jesus sets his face to head to Jerusalem and fulfil his calling as the suffering servant who would lay down his life as a ransom for many.

More painful than the brute spiritual blindness of the general populace and the religious is the lack of perception of his own disciples. He comes down the mountain back to another overheated crowd, another set of religious opponents and also to the failure of his disciples. They can't do what they've been doing successfully up until now; they can't cast out a demon (Mark 9:17). They throw away their spiritual confidence or faith. Jesus says, *"Everything is possible for him who believes"* (9:23).

But not for those whose heads are turned by the crowd and the disapproval of the religious.

The boy's father speaks for himself and the disciples, you feel, when he protests, *"I do believe, help me overcome my unbelief!"* (9:24).

When we pray for people, we are sometimes dealing with the

effects of friendly fire – wounds that our own side have inflicted on people i.e. other Christians have disappointed us and let us down. *Let us reason together; all Christians are a tremendous disappointment!*

We are like second hand cars: by definition, not as good as new cars. Don't be deterred by the disappointing behaviour of other believers, because sooner or later it will be matched by your own. Forgive and move on. I write this glibly for effect, but I know that sometimes this involves quite a process.

After Jesus was baptised, he was led by the Spirit into the desert where he was tempted by the devil and the focus at that time was on his identity: *"If you are the Son of God"* (Matthew 41-11). After the Transfiguration though, there is no point in calling his identity into question and so the devil changes tack. Now it's about whether his mission is working or not. "Look", says Satan (who cannot prevent what has happened on the Mountain) "the crowd have no idea what's going on, the leaders are becoming more antagonistic and even your own people don't get it. It's not working is it?"

Ever thought, "What I believed God wanted me to do isn't working"? Why not just give up"?

So the combined effects of the brutality of human beings, the censure of religious people, and the disappointment of being let down by our own team is to a) prevent us living out our true identity as sons and daughters of God and, if that horse has bolted, b) to call into question what we are doing for God.

If your parents or other significant people have not given you a sense of worth, how could God love you? If you still carry such and such a wound from the past, how can God use you? If your good intentions have been so misjudged, how will you carry on doing what God wants you to do? How can this be God when it is so difficult?

The devil is behind all of this and more.

He often uses the way things are in the fallen world to tell us the lies of the land. And he reveals his destructive nature in the victimisation of the demonised people we meet in the Gospels, including a little boy (Mark 9:14f). He can't speak, is thrown around, foams at the mouth and gnashes his teeth. The spirit has tried to kill the boy using fire and water. Jesus tell us, *"The thief comes to kill, steal and destroy"* (John 10:10).

The disciples want to know why their efforts to cast out the spirit failed (Mark 9:28). Jesus says *"This kind only comes out by prayer"* (9:29). I believe this is a reference back to the kind of spiritual authority and power that comes from the unseen foundations of his life, including prayer. The kinds of damages inflicted on us come out in response to the prayers of those who are obedient, dwell in the love of God and are filled with the Spirit. This is how we find healing for the hurts we have suffered, for the religious abuse we have experienced, for the disappointment we have endured and for the direct attacks of the devil. Blessed are those who offer such healing in Jesus' name because this is what he did.

We can be so used to the lies of the land that the Christian life doesn't especially feel like a battle. But that is only because we have been lulled into a false sense of security. In reality, all Christians are at war, whether they want to be or not. So I suggest we do all we can to embrace our identity as sons and daughters, enter into our calling as followers of Christ, and give no room for the devil by finding healing where we need it. Let us also go on the offensive, taking off the grave clothes of others, declaring the year of the Lord's favour, and the nearness of his Kingdom over people's lives, for we know that *"Where the Spirit of the Lord is, there is freedom"* (2 Corinthians 3:17).

Inner Healing And Deliverance

Inner healing is bringing God's healing to past hurts, whereas *deliverance* is bringing God's freedom from demonic influence. So obviously, we don't want to use deliverance language ("I bind you/

get out in Jesus' name") in inner healing contexts (problems of sin/ hurtful situations from the past). Confusion arises because Satan can use past hurts or damaging patterns of behaviour against us and because many Christians interested in this area don't distinguish properly between the human and the spiritual.

Inner Healing

- All Christians have died to the past: *"Don't you know that all of you who were baptised into Christ were baptised into his death"* (Romans 6:3).
- But all Christians must daily die to themselves: *"You were taught with regard to your former way of life to put off the old nature, which is being corrupted by sinful desires, to be made new in the attitude of your minds and put on the new nature created to be like God in righteousness."* (Ephesians 4:22-23)
- All the resources we need to live an integrated Christian life are available to us in Jesus, but we must choose to walk in them or put them on.
- So inner healing isn't endlessly wallowing around in something that happened in the past, neither is it deliverance from demons.
- It is finding the freedom Jesus brings from attitudes, beliefs and practices that characterised us before we came to Christ, and that are incompatible with our new identity in him e.g. addictive patterns of behaviour or harmful images of God mediated to us by our parents. This is a life-long process.

How are we set free?

- We need to re-orientate our world view, replacing our parents' influence, upbringing, environment and experiences with the teaching of the Bible and our experience of God as the new standard of rationality. We can help people with this when we pray for them. The most significant areas are a person's view of the character of God and of themselves in relation to God.

- This re-orientation is a process and when we pray for people we are helping them make the journey. People in ministry times are often in the process of identifying unbiblical views, facing up to what has happened in the past and trying to deal with what comes up, before embracing a new way of seeing what has happened and themselves in relation to it in the light of what Jesus has done for them.

- This process may require the removal of specific road blocks: the healing of particular memories, the release or receiving of forgiveness, the release of pain or anger and acts of reconciliation outside of the ministry context. This is where we come in. Everyone is somewhere on this journey; no one has arrived.

- Apart from people who can minister in the power of the Spirit, people may also need the help of specialists like doctors and therapists and also an on-going experience of healthy church relationships.

Example X

Presenting problems: becoming cynical about his Christian experience and unsure of God's love.

Below the surface: his father was not physically intimate during his childhood, never forgave him if he made a mistake and couldn't be trusted.

Behaviour: use of homosexual porn (his father had insisted he should never be gay), an inability to talk about personal things, a dichotomy between his beliefs and his feelings, an inability to accept forgiveness and a stifling attitude to relationships.

Process: a series of sessions helping to reveal the true scope of his issues, receiving insight that explained why he behaved as he did, praying for the healing of memories of painful episodes from his life and the correcting of unbiblical views. I also had a useful prophetic word whilst thinking, "This isn't working." I felt God say, "Tell him he is like a bird with broken wings. That will speak to him." This impression came from "left field" and I didn't initially trust it. I thought the word sounded too emotional for him. However, when I finally said it, he told me that he had always thought of himself as being like a bird with broken wings and had only felt free when watching birds fly. So this word spoke to him and showed him that God knew him. This greatly assisted the healing process.

* * *

I would say the following is a typical story of personal brokenness and illustrates how healing often comes over time:

"I grew up stuttering. When it began I do not know, but it continued throughout my formative years and well into my late thirties. At school, I was taunted, laughed at and ridiculed by my peers for my attempts at speaking. Stuttering caused ticking which caused facial distortions. Stamping my feet and tapping my head were coping mechanisms I developed to help get the words out. I hated my life then with the constant mockery. It was very painful. I did not participate in public speaking or group debates.

As a child I was given water beaten with pestle and mortar to drink which, apparently, would 'cure' the problem. I drank this water for many days, weeks, and years but the stuttering continued.

Whilst attending college, my maths teacher took it upon himself to organise an appointment with a speech therapist for me without consulting me first. 'How dare he!' I thought. 'I won't go!' During a math lesson, he challenged me in front of the entire class about my obstinacy and being a coward in not wanting to attend the speech therapy sessions he had organised. I could not defend myself, lest I started to stutter and the embarrassment of the whole class staring at me. I was overcome with rage and left the classroom in floods of tears. I went to my first speech therapy session that afternoon and once a week for about 3 months. If people thought I was a freak, then I would be classed a human robot now because the speech therapist's technique was based on speaking syllabically which made me sounded like a robot. I decided I would rather stutter than speak like a robot! I stopped attending the sessions.

I grew up in foster care and went to church twice on Sundays – Sunday School in the morning and church in the evening – as part of my upbringing. I had no choice! Did I know God or become a Christian as a result of that over-churching? NO. The God I was introduced to was not one I could get to know, let alone have a relationship with. He was a God of fire and brimstone and I was petrified of him!

In my late teens I started to attend church on my own terms and not because I had no choice. My life was still traumatic and I wanted to find solace. I began to pray that God would heal my stuttering, thus proving himself to me as a God of miracles and one who loves, cares and understands the constant pain and ridicule from the people who were always laughing at me and making me feel stupid. My parents abandoned me at age 2 and it felt like God had abandoned me too, because he was not answering my prayer for healing. I didn't give up praying though, for all the good it did.

During a prayer meeting one Sunday, I prayed my most earnest prayer that God would heal my stuttering and set me free from what had become a bondage all these years. Through many tears during that prayer time, I distinctly felt something different: I felt like an elastic band had stretched to capacity within me and returned to normal. From that moment I believed I had been healed of my stuttering.

Did I suddenly stop stuttering and begin speaking normally? NO. My stuttering continued, but gradually I began to notice a difference. I was not stuttering all the time anymore. I was more open to participate in group discussions without the fear of stuttering. Friends and families who grew up seeing me stuttering are amazed that I now speak without a stutter. I am a normal person now, speaking without a stutter and enjoying my life."

Deliverance

- It is worth noting these descriptions of Jesus' ministry: *"Since the children have flesh and blood, he too shared in their humanity so that by his death he might destroy him who holds the power of death – that is the devil - and free those who all their lives were held in slavery"* (Hebrews 2:14-15) and *"the reason the Son of God appeared was to destroy the devil's work"* (1 John 3:8).

- The New Testament teaches the existence of Satan and demons (Luke 10:17, 20).

- Jesus' ministry was full of confrontations with demons (Luke 4:31-37).

- The New Testament is clear about Jesus' authority over demons: *"be strong in the Lord and his mighty power. Put on the full armor of God so that you can take your stand against the devil's schemes. For our struggle is not against flesh and blood but against the rulers, authorities and powers of this dark world"* (Ephesians 6:10-12); *"And having disarmed the powers and authorities he made a public spectacle of them, triumphing over them by the cross"* (Colossians 2:5).

- Clearly, as well, Jesus delegated authority over demons to his disciples: *"The 72 came back with great joy; 'Lord, even the demons submit to us in your name.' He replied, 'I saw Satan fall like lightning from heaven. I have given you authority to trample on scorpions and snakes and to overcome all the works of the evil one'"* (Luke 10:17-20).

- The origins of Satan, how or why he exists, is not explained with any clarity. The consensus is that he was a fallen angel who rejected God and led an angelic rebellion against him. Throughout church history, Christians have borne witness to confrontations with the demonic.

- Demons are intelligent (Acts 16:16), manifest in different forms (Revelation 13), are malevolent (Matthew 12:43), have supernatural power (Matthew 12:29) and know their end (Matthew 8:29).

Here are some well-tried demonic tactics:

Direct assault: An attempt to take us out of the picture through actual or threatened violence. Satan inspires persecution, usually accompanied by gross misrepresentations of the faith, trumped up charges, and gross injustices.

Accusation or indirect assault: An attempt to overwhelm us and stop us doing what we are doing for God by a flood of lies told against us. These can come from within or outside the church. Cleverly, there is often an element of truth in what is thrown at us, focusing perhaps on real faults or mistakes and/or reflecting the real failings of the people involved. This includes a constant caricaturing of the church as a pathetic, useless relic that will never be able to help anyone.

Condemnation: An attempt to take us out of the game caused by demonic reminders of weaknesses and sins, which can lead to a pervasive sense of failure and despair. These are flaming darts of the evil one intended to neutralise us. It is very important that we learn how to use the shield of faith, indeed all the armour of God (Ephesians 6:10-18). For instance, it is normal to experience a sense of shame and regret about sins we have committed. However, it is vital that we learn how to receive forgiveness, to close off the potential for condemnation and inaction that will otherwise be exploited.

Counterfeit: An attempt to discredit genuine movements of the Spirit by offering false versions which call these into question and deceive some Christians, blowing them off course. This is where

Satan appears *"as an angel of light"* (2 Corinthians 11:14), seducing religious people with the doctrine of demons. This has been at play since the start when Satan quickly offered alternatives to the Spirit-empowered early church either through Gnostic or Jewish legalistic heresies. False religion is very close in appearance to Christianity and only works for this reason. This kind of thing, which finds its expression in such cults as the Jehovah's Witnesses or the Mormons for instance, is very different from the disagreements that exist between Christians on points of doctrine.

Temptation: An attempt to bring about an on-going state of defeat in our lives. The devil aims to exploit specific weaknesses personal to us with a view to compromising our witness and rendering us inactive. I would put in this category as well the more difficult to detect temptation to live a sub-Christian life, reflecting materialistic, classist, racist, sexist, homophobic attitudes or the middle-class aspirations of the culture of which we are a part.

Demonisation: This is an attempt to mock God's work by taking a measure of control over something created by him for his glory, usually a human being. The expression "possessed by demons" isn't found in New Testament Greek and actually reflects English concepts of property ownership, which were incorporated into the King's James version of the Bible. "Demonisation" is a better term and the expression means "coming under the influence of a demon or demons" – something that can be experienced internally or externally depending on how severe the case is. Only some of the people seeming to need deliverance actually do. Others have genuine needs, but not for deliverance from evil spirits. Other issues they might really need help with include emotional hurt, an unhealthy obsession with evil, an unhealthy obsession with deliverance, unresolved guilt or mental disturbance. If someone tells you they are possessed, they rarely are!

Here are the classic tests of demonic control:

- A fearful or aggressive response to the things of God in general and Jesus in particular e.g. the cross, the communion or the presence of the Spirit.

- Behaviour out of keeping with the known personality of the person you are praying for. This is one of several reasons why it is good to have someone present who knows the person you are praying for.

- Supernatural power e.g. extraordinary strength, knowledge and voices speaking through the person. It is absolutely crucial to recognise that some unusual manifestations could be indicative of mental disturbance. Where there is a suspicion that such may be the case, it is good to have some awareness of the person's medical history and even to know what a doctor thinks about their symptoms. Where there is doubt about whether what is happening could be the result of mental disturbance, it is sensible to see if medical treatment works. If it doesn't then it might be good to explore deliverance. The Bible offers no hard and fast rules for determining the presence of a demon. In general, they are panicked into revealing themselves in the presence of Jesus. Some Christians have a gift of discerning Spirits that can make this process easier. I spoke to a woman recently about her regular experience of a sweet smell in a room when the Holy Spirit is present, versus a foul one when she meets a demonised person. All totally subjective, of course.

Entry Points

- *Occult involvement:* those involved in various forms of the occult (e.g. tarot, Ouija, spiritualism) prior to conversion need prayer to break the power of any remaining influence. We don't need to actively seek the influence of the demonic to become influenced by it, in the same way that we don't need to know we are walking through tar to get it on our shoes. Some people can be seriously demonised through only a slight involvement in an occult practice whilst others are hardly affected at all.

- *Past hurts:* this is only speculation on my part, but I wonder if these can create the potential for greater demonic interference if the damage is severe enough? Imagine our inner person being surrounded by a protective shell made up of all the positive experiences that aid our development as healthy human beings. If there are sufficiently serious cracks in that shell, I theorise that, if we then expose ourselves to spiritual power outside of Christ, this can result in demonisation.

- *Sinful patterns of behaviour:* all sins are the result of demonic temptation, but that does not mean that demons swoop down and enter us every time we sin. But repeating patterns of failure can be further exploited as described above and again, I theorise that if we already have cracks in the core of our personhood through damages of one kind or another, this may leave us at greater risk of demonic influence and control.

The presence of the above may be signals, but are never proofs of demonic influence. Not everyone who comes for prayer with these problems is demonised. We always need to proceed with caution and I am only really willing to call something demonic when it is reasonably obvious that this is what we are dealing with. For instance, a colleague of mine was preparing to pray for someone who appeared to be demonised. He lacked experience and spent a bit of time looking at himself in the mirror, asking if he was really ready for this. When he started to pray for the person a few minutes later, a voice spoke out of her saying, "I saw you looking in the mirror."

It was a bit of a give-away, wasn't it?

Demons sometimes show themselves and leave immediately during ministry time, especially if there is a lot of power. If you think this is happening, command anything afflicting the person to leave in Jesus' name. When you are praying for someone and there appears to be a bit of a struggle going on, ask questions like, "Does this feel bad/is this a struggle/are you in pain in your body/have you been involved in the occult ever or have your family?"

Be gentle.

If it is demonic, people often feel pain in the chest, stomach or throat and demons leave as we command them to in Jesus' name with a cough, scream or vomit. Usually the person appears to be removed from what is happening. This is because the demon is manifesting at this time. If the process is on-going, always take the person off to a private setting and continue from there. We never need to rush into a deliverance. It is possible to shut everything down and meet at another time.

- Always pray with several people present so that what happens cannot be misrepresented. It is good for one to lead and a couple of others to support and pray.
- Always respect the dignity of the person.
- Unless the demon leaves straight away, we need to know the likely entry point or cause of the demonisation. When people repent of their prior involvement in the occult, the demon has no right to stay.
- We command the demon to leave in Jesus' name.
- We don't need to know its name, but we do often need to know how it got in.
- We stop when the person is free and pray for them to be filled with the Spirit; sometimes you need more than one session.
- Always make sure there are people there with previous experience.
- The person affected needs to get rid of anything associated – like occult books – or the demons can return.
- They often feel exhausted afterwards and may not remember

much of what happened. Check in on them the next day.

- In a time of ministry, when there are more experienced people about, they will know if a demon is manifesting and should get involved and take over from less experienced team members. Let them do this but pray and worship, watch and learn.
- Don't lead this kind of ministry if you are a young Christian or new to things of the Spirit.

True story

"I moved to a 'house share' with people who attended St Mary's. I went there, soon felt at home and signed up for their Alpha course. This was my second course and I enjoyed the deepening of my faith and set off for the weekend away. During the time of prayer on the Saturday, I felt strong physical sensations – but none were any different from those I had felt on my first weekend away. The stomach burping and growling was, though, clearly audible. When a particular member of the team prayed for me and placed his hand on my stomach, my reaction became more intense for a while before subsiding. I felt that intuitively, this person had known exactly where to go in my body to administer healing. I was also struck by the biblical words which he had quoted to me during the healing prayer, where the Lord declares, *"I will repay you for the years the locusts have eaten"* (Joel 2:25).

On the Sunday morning, I had breakfast with a young woman whom I really liked and was enjoying getting to know. Suddenly an involuntary sensation came over me. I was looking at her but having the image of harming her in the eyes. When we left the table, I went to my room, fell to my knees, wept bitterly and spoke to God. I said that I bore no ill will to this young woman, I only wanted to enjoy friendship with her, but that something was coming between us that was not "me". I pleaded with God to deliver me from this feeling once and for all during the next session, which was due to start in twenty minutes. I felt that this was a disturbing legacy from my past and that I might need to have a "messy" session and told myself that I should not feel inhibited or stop anything from happening that needed to happen.

I went downstairs and the Holy Spirit session started. Within a few minutes, the member of the prayer team from the previous day returned and placed his hand directly on my stomach. Instantly, I was filled with anger, even rage, although I wasn't actually feeling these emotions myself. It was like something else "inside me" was feeling them and I was simply an observer. Then I began growling, baring my teeth. I heard another person coming towards me and realised, as he started praying, that it was the leader of the prayer team. He placed a hand on my head and began praying, ordering the evil spirit to depart.

Within myself I felt relaxed and relieved. At last, things were coming to a head. I could feel something inside me continuing to rise in opposition to the two people praying. However, I could observe this happening, even enjoy the experience of knowing that some kind of catharsis was occurring. My body was filled with streams of angry, flowing energy, but I felt in control and that I just needed to stay on the touchline of this battle and let it take place without interfering.

Meanwhile, I began bowing my head forward, lowering it to the floor until I was hunched up and crouching over. It was an animal posture. My face felt like a wild boar's, baring its teeth. I thought that other people would probably be watching and getting distracted from their own prayer, but I knew that I had to let things ride their course. Part of me continued to behave like an animal and grow more hostile – and then suddenly the feeling went. Those praying for me had ordered the spirit to depart – not with any great emotion or struggle, simply with a decisive authority in the name of Jesus Christ.

I began to return to an upright position. People continued to pray for me to be filled with the Holy Spirit, especially in the inner places vacated by the evil spirit. I felt waves of the Holy Spirit streaming into me, felt jubilant at being released, and spontaneously lifted my hands high in the air in praise to God. I must have spent at least another ten minutes in this position, filled with awe and love for God. I felt ecstatic, filled with joy of a kind and intensity I'd never experienced before.

I was totally released. We returned to London and since that time I have had no further repetition of those involuntary experiences. For the first time, I understood what the word "deliverance" really meant."

14
Worship

The Vineyard not only gave us a model for ministry in the power of the Spirit, but also demonstrated a way of worshipping that was congruent with it. This continues to be of interest to me because worship without space for the expression of spiritual gifts is, in my view, unbiblical. We assume that early patterns of worship were based on the Jewish inheritance and that most churches met in people's homes. There is precious little additional information about the worship life of the early church in the New Testament other than what we read in 1 Corinthians. But here it is obvious that the expression of the gifts played a prominent role. As has been previously noted, the Corinthians made all manner of mistakes, but Paul does not discourage the expression of the gifts of the Spirit. On the contrary, he expected the Corinthians to use them when they met together for worship, but to do so in an orderly fashion.

John Wimber described a journey of worship. He pointed out that in the temple in Jerusalem, anyone was allowed to enter the outer courts, whether they were part of the people of God or not. But only the people of God could enter the inner courts and only the High Priest could enter the Holy of Holies. Wimber encouraged the writing of contemporary worship songs to help people move from "the outer courts" of praise to "the Holy of Holies" of worship. Jesus, our great High Priest, has gone ahead of us into the presence of the Father and in him, we have the privilege of doing the same (Hebrews 4:14-16).

The songs we sing should help us make this journey.

- *Praise songs* (the outer courts): songs that are more objective, describing the character of God and acknowledging the corporate nature of what we are doing. This includes songs that remind us of what we have come here to do, in which we sing to each other as well as directly to God. In a way, anyone could listen in – and maybe even join in - without feeling too uncomfortable.

- *Worship songs* (the inner courts): songs that could only be sung with integrity by those who consider themselves to be worshippers of Jesus. Songs directed to God, declaring our faith in him and our thankfulness to him for all he has done for us.
- *Love songs* (the Holy of Holies): short refrains which enable us to give expression to the depths of our love for God.

Finding ourselves in a shared state of intimate vulnerability before God is the goal of corporate worship.

Singing in tongues, in which together we express the deepest mysteries and cries of our inner beings is the natural "high point" in this experience of connection.

After we have poured out our hearts to God, it is our privilege to hear God speak to us. This is where prophecy comes in with its character of encouragement and comfort. As Paul explains, that God speaks is the most important sign that God is with us when we meet together.

I heard that the leader of one of our plants was having trouble deciding whether to interrupt the flow of prophetic words and stories of answers to prayer in order to preach. I suspected in my cynical way that this might be an evangelist's flourish of the kind I would be guilty of myself. However, when I next visited the church, I found that it wasn't.

Originally, the church had met in a very poor part of town, in a Christian drug rehab centre. None of the original planting team lived in this area, but they came to love the people who did. They were grieved when they were asked to leave. Some members of the church went back to the neighbourhood after the church had been re-established in a more affluent area. They set up a table offering water and food to local people. A doctor felt the Spirit prompt her to offer free medical care in a vacant house behind the table. She was unwilling to do this without confirmation. The next Sunday, a word of knowledge was given about someone offering medical care behind the table. She responded. Soon, teams of people went in to pray for people on the streets and in their homes. Then they set up a prayer meeting to support all that was happening.

When I was there, people in the service literally ran to the front to have the chance to tell a story about what God had just done. They developed a "prophecy wall" so people could write their words on a board, since there wasn't time to hear all the words that people wanted to give in a service. Hence, the leader's preaching dilemma. I always say to my worship leaders, "Give me a problem; let it be difficult for me to end the worship and prophecy time for fear of getting in the way of what God is doing."

None of which means I undervalue the power of preaching. It's just that it should be the Holy Spirit who ultimately leads our service and he doesn't always rigidly adhere to our plans or timetable.

So worship is first of all a spiritual activity.

I pray for next Sunday's service from Monday onwards, always inviting the Holy Spirit to come and fill the building, the service leader, the worship leader, the band, the speaker and the ministry team. And I pray that the Spirit will touch everyone who comes – those who belong and those who don't yet.

Worship is also a human activity.

For instance, how do the leaders of the service feel about what they are doing today and how do the people feel about being there? Is it too cold, too hot, too loud, too quiet, too professional, too controlled, too unprofessional, too relaxed, insensitive, over-sensitive?

Worship is a process.

Are the songs we are singing, is the way this service is being led, actually helping us go on the journey together? In reality, most people are comparatively disconnected from God when they start to worship. We are mainly aware of the other people around us and the environment we are in. As time goes by, as we embark on the journey, we usually become more aware of ourselves, how we are feeling about things that have happened and more aware of God. Our desire is to feel deeply connected to God, aware of ourselves in relation to him and aware of ourselves as fellow worshippers. This includes becoming open to the gifts of the Spirit. Does God want to use us in some way or speak to us, or do something in us through the ministry of others?

No No's

Song lyrics define Christian theological understanding more than anything else. Of course, it ought to be personal Bible study and teaching, but it isn't. I believe we should avoid these lyrical categories:

- "God is sending you suffering and he's a bit cross with you" lyrics. The most important truth to glean from the New Testament is that God is nice and he likes us. This is the revelation that leads to worship. Because most Christian songwriters have not studied theology and are subject to no one who has, erroneous ideas about God can creep in. Old Testament ideas about the way God works in the world or amongst his people are especially popular. Although Jesus spent his entire ministry taking away suffering, Christian lyricists are sometimes keen on the idea that God is refining us or making us more like him by making us suffer.

This isn't true.

- "Jesus is my boyfriend" lyrics. I know this will come as a tremendous disappointment to many Christians, but the Song of Songs is actually an erotic love poem and in the original Hebrew, rather sexually explicit. It belongs to the literary genre known as "wisdom", which comprises content not directly about God, but is still worth having. We are not meant to extract from this text the idea that God is our "beautiful one". We are meant to deduce that eroticism is an important ingredient in a marriage. In our culture, to fall in love is to have a strong romantic/erotic attraction to another person. We are not called to get all romantic with God. You know how men don't tend to go to church in the UK? Given that romance with a woman is challenging enough for most of them anyway, I wonder if we have found a reason why they don't like our kind of church? Adoration language, yes; falsely borrowed erotic language, no thanks.

- "This is terrible English and largely incomprehensible but it's prophetic" lyrics. I really, really want to give an example but I shouldn't. OK, just one. During the Toronto Blessing someone wrote a song entitled, "Jumbo, double, double – Holy Spirit, come down." Facile, twee, incomprehensible or reprehensible language deadens the Christian soul. Also "prophetic" does not mean "grammatically or theologically incorrect" or "unchallengeable".

- "I'd like to teach you a few things" songs. Worship leaders are meant to lead worship, whilst teachers are meant to teach. Let me do my job and I promise not to touch your guitar. Avoid songs that are basically imparting a worship leader's thoughts on what the church should be doing Monday to Saturday.

- "It's all about me but I could probably use a bit of God to make me even more amazing" lyrics. If the lyrics describe a person who very much believes in their potential, but isn't averse to a bit of God on the side, I would ditch it. I know we desperately want everything in life to be about us, but worship is, by definition, actually focused on someone else.

In fact, I already know enough about me when I come to worship. I have been living with the reality of me all week. What I need when I come to church is someone to fill my mind with a vision of God.

Give us songs that describe the greatness and power of God and help us see ourselves in relation to him. In some songs, it isn't clear who we are actually singing about – could be God, could be someone else we are in relationship with. Is this because we are hoping to "cross over" into the secular market? It all feels a bit self-related, but this is what happens when there hasn't been a significant movement of the Spirit recently. In his absence, we tend to turn in on ourselves. *Let's not.*

What is a good worship leader like?
You'd get the impression that they have to be...

- ...15-22 year's old
- cool
- attractive
- a brilliant singer
- a brilliant musician
- a brilliant songwriter
- incapable of looking directly at a camera if having their photo taken because they are just so self-effacing
- nevertheless interested in a humble way in becoming a very successful recording artist.

In reality, they need to be...

- ...a person of the Spirit, who has experienced the Spirit and knows how the Spirit moves in a worship context.
- a person who really loves worship and enjoys leading people.
- a person who is humble, teachable and willing to work with other Spirit-filled leaders.

- a person who refuses to allow immature Christians to project their culturally derived celebrity fixation onto them just because they can play the guitar and stand on a stage without falling off.
- a person who is willing to work on any areas of their craft that might be weaker, though deficiencies in these areas won't stop God using them.

Some of the best worship leaders I have known have not been particularly good singers or musicians and have written no songs. But they love worship, have no concerns about leading people in worship, and know how to interpret what the Spirit is doing. But just as it makes sense if you speak regularly to have a vision for becoming better at all aspects of speaking, it is good to have a vision for growing in all aspects of worship leading, including musicianship.

It's actually unusual for a worship leader to be a brilliant singer, musician and songwriter. If this is a career path, it's one that not many are truly gifted to pursue. Why not just be a worship leader and see what happens?

True story

"I hadn't been committed to any church for about 10 years. The time at my previous church had left me disillusioned and deeply hurt, though I never lost my faith. I'm a singer and was a worship leader and I had continued to worship the Lord at home throughout those years. My piano was a place of refuge, and I would sing and weep and process all the disappointment I felt. I had also become very ill with a degenerative kidney disease which had no cure.

So when I came through the doors at St Mary's I was very broken. I didn't want anyone to notice me, I just wanted to sneak in unseen and leave straight away afterwards. I had been the week before and I came back because I was so hungry for the Holy Spirit and I had felt his presence so strongly.

After the service had just begun, John came up to me and asked, "Will you trust me?" I didn't understand why until afterwards. The question John asked about trust was God getting to the heart of the matter straight away. Here was the leader of the church, someone who represented everything that had been so hurtful to me in the past, asking me if I would trust him. I knew I had to make a decision, and I said yes.

The reason John asked me that was because the Holy Spirit had told him to call me out in front of the whole church and tell me publicly that God loved my voice. John had never heard me sing and so was understandably reluctant to do so, but he did!

I was called out to the front of the church and I heard God communicate to me that I was seen and known and loved by Him. That all those years of weeping and singing at my piano were precious to him, and he loved to hear me sing. I was also prayed for and encouraged as a worship leader. But that wasn't the end of it, God also told John that I was in financial need, which was true. I had had to give up work due to illness and my husband and I were in a lot of debt. The church then provided us with an incredible financial gift which was so unexpected and such a blessing to us.

I had been trying to run away and hide for years. I took a tentative step forward and God met me with a tidal wave of love. Over the last four years, God has healed my heart so profoundly, he has provided for us time and time again. We are now debt free and my health has improved dramatically.

I am so grateful to God for his faithfulness, kindness and love. I am also grateful to John for taking a risk that day and being obedient to the voice of the Holy Spirit. I honestly would have run away again if God had not spoken to me so clearly. I'm so glad he did, because it changed my life and gave me hope again."

15
Leading Ministry

If you are a leader or someone who already knows and practices the model of ministry described in this book, I would strongly encourage you to start leading times of ministry yourself, if you get the opportunity. It's like praying for one person really, so you will already be familiar with much of what is involved.

By way of preparation, in addition to encouraging us to pay attention to the unseen foundations described in chapter eight, I want to draw attention to a few other things that might help us get ready.

Prayer

It is amazing that we try to get by without prayer, but I guess this is further proof that *the blatantly obvious isn't always obvious to people like us.* When Jesus likens us to sheep, that is not a compliment, for sheep will gather in the same part of a field even if there is a snow drift in that very place. We with sheep-like stupidity underestimate the importance of prayer. If we want to lead ministry – or just aim to keep in step with the Spirit in our day to day lives – we need to pray.

I like things to be as humane and as easy as possible so, I suggest that if you work for a church, you should consider prayer to be part of your job, whether you are praying on your own or with others. All Christians need the guidance of God in their lives, but if full-time Christian workers aren't going beyond the hard won ten minutes of the office worker at the start of the day, or the last thing at night five minutes of the exhausted mother, the well of inspiration is quickly going to run dry and we won't be leading anyone very far.

So let's think, "I am paid to pray."

There have been many times when I have tried to write a sermon without any idea where to begin and have floundered around hopelessly. By contrast, after prayer, I often find that such things write themselves.

Sailing the boat is easy when you catch the wind. To catch the wind, you have to be on the sea. To be on the sea, you have to get off the shore.

I think that analogy has blown away now.

To pray is to enjoy the presence, nearness, voice, comfort, affirmation and reassurance of God. Why would we ever shy away from this experience, prioritising anything above prayer?

I know the many answers as well as you do. It's because...

- ...we have children
- we didn't sleep
- we are worried
- we've sinned
- we've made things too complicated
- we don't sense these things when we pray
- we somehow feel we are working for God, not simply enjoying our relationship with him
- we are angry or disappointed with God
- we've lost touch with the fundamental faith statement that I am following someone else's agenda and not my own
- we have somehow come to believe that it is all up to us.

Does this sound familiar?

With all the pressures we face, either in our leadership or in everyday life, the processing of our deepest concerns and needs is meant to happen in prayer. And it is the continuous act of coming to God for our truest experience of connection that helps us separate,

- our inner voice
- from the voices of others who shape us

- from the voice of the Spirit.

We held an event one summer for the regular givers of the church. It was intended to be a "thank you for all you have given", but we developed a deficit, so it became a thank you plus an appeal for more money. In the morning, I lost confidence about asking for money. Then in the afternoon, whilst I was praying, I felt the Holy Spirit interrupt and ask me about my original intentions for the event. I had wanted to show everyone just how much of an impact their giving had made over the years, to thank them and to ask them to support new aspects of our vision. I felt God say, "Why don't you ask for a lot of money, then? Ask one person to give £15K, ask two people to give £10K and several to give £5K; then give away everything else away."

Based on previous experience, I felt this was probably God.

So I didn't say anything to anyone, except I commented nervously to a few friends, "This is either going to go incredibly well or incredibly badly. Please pray!" After the presentation, I thanked the people for trusting me over the years when I had claimed that I was being led by the Spirit and then told them what I felt God had asked me to do – to meet the deficit first then give everything else away. I asked everyone to close their eyes.

Anyone feel they should give £15K? (No one).

Anyone £10K? (Several).

Anyone £5k (Several).

We passed our deficit, which was about £35K. I then asked everyone else to give or pledge and in the end the people there that evening gave £120K. This included a minority of very wealthy people and a lot of people who aren't. They all understand the power of giving.

Let's think about this for a moment.

I could have been guided by my own voice, which is concerned about asking for money.

I could have been guided by the voices of my colleagues who also felt for perfectly good reasons that it might not be wise to ask for money.

I am grateful to God that on this occasion I followed his voice. The difference was £120k versus £0K.

When we pray, let's adopt a "without an agenda" approach. We all have lots of things we need to pray about, but prayer as a means of connection with God is the most important. This is because when I actually believe I am who Jesus says I am, more can happen through me. "Our Father in heaven", "Hallowed be thy name", "They Kingdom come", "Thy will be done on earth, as it is in heaven" come first in the Lord's Prayer. This means that expressions of adoration, intimacy, praise and alignment come before requests for ourselves and other people.

Living life decided

Under pressure to succeed, to please people, to get everything right, we can sideline the Spirit's agenda. What would you point to as evidence that you are actually trying to follow the Spirit in your work, family life, or church leadership? Of course, everyone needs a plan, but we can be so committed to our plan that we don't appear to need God.

Sorry, no, we need him to bless our plan!

This presupposes that we know more than we do about how to get things done or indeed about what is going to happen. I remind us that Jesus only did what he saw the Father doing and he discerned that by the power of the Spirit. He only had a plan in general terms – to go throughout the towns and villages of Israel, proclaiming the Kingdom. He relied on the direction of the Spirit for the details.

Jesus' ministry could easily be characterised as a series of disruptions or apparent diversions from the plan. If we want to move in the Spirit, as opposed to doing our best and hoping that will do, we have to hold lightly to everything we plan. We have to become responsive, able to sense when the wind is changing direction. We have to be willing to disregard all else if we think God is asking us to.

I decided I wasn't going to a Christian event recently. There are things about it I didn't like. This led to conflict with the relational wife who likes it. God showed me very clearly that he wanted me to go by means of separate conversations in which three people who know me well expressed the same home truth about me to my face.

This was something I didn't want to hear.

Now it's one thing to be reluctant to do something and to actively make other plans.

We all do that.

It's another thing to stick to our plan when God is clearly asking us to depart from it. Of course, he continually has mercy on us in our weakness, but whenever we do this we miss something amazing – just as I would have done at the fundraising event. I subsequently discovered that my contribution to this event led to a lot of people receiving the ministry they needed. This suggests to me that God's interest in the people coming to this event was greater than his interest in my concerns about going to the event.

How could that be?!

Connect with other people of the Spirit

I was greatly helped in the early days of my leadership by many people who knew more about the ways of the Spirit than I did. I started to lead at a time of spiritual plenty in England. It was easy to contact Vineyard pastors as well and to go to conferences. I advise you to hold onto anyone you know who is further down the road in the ministry of the Spirit than you are. This also applies to people who are trying to follow the Spirit as you are. They will both inspire and refresh you.

Also, in so far as you possibly can, raise up people of the Spirit and pass on what you know. We actually receive most when we give away most, something that is hard for us to really believe. This particularly applies to the investment we make in the lives of younger leaders. But if church leaders do their jobs properly, it won't be a one-way street in which their young leaders do all the taking. As the people we mentor start to truly express their spiritual gifts, the whole church benefits and sometimes we find that we have created a spiritual monster who can really help us carry weight. I encouraged a couple called James and Janie Cronin and a very young worship leader called Chris Jones to go and help set up our first church plant in Auckland, New Zealand. Not only did they do a brilliant job there, but they then went on to help another leader establish a plant in Jacksonville, Florida. They have carried the burden with me of many of the planting initiatives we have taken. At one stage though, James and Janie weren't Christians and Chris was simply a young musician who moved to London to pursue his career.

Who do you know that is open to the Spirit that you could invest in?

I look for people who are already *showing the signs*, who've already been bitten. Some leaders have told me, "It is hard to raise up leaders here." I'm sure some contexts are more challenging than others, but I wonder whether it is the level of investment needed to really see someone emerge that deters some leaders from helping the next generation? Or maybe some are afraid that if they do this they will be admitting that passing on what they know is now their most valuable contribution? I was late to the mentoring party and only started because I couldn't get rid of a young leader called Mike Norris. But here was a man who was very open to the Spirit, was an evangelist, was funny and intelligent, and quickly good at what he did. How difficult was it to spend time with someone like that? Not very.

I have enjoyed the mentoring process with most of the people who have trained under my leadership – the only exceptions being those who avoided my advice and refused to face obvious barriers to their personal growth. There is obviously a disparity between our calling and gifts, which are real, and our capacity to fulfil our calling and exercise our gifts, which the immature leader cannot fully do due to inexperience and unresolved things that make the flow of the Spirit difficult in their lives.

What young leaders need and deserve is help as they go through the process. But this takes time and can be a messy and involves a "two steps forward one step back" sort of progression. But if we don't raise up future Spirit people, the burden will be too great on existing leaders. Jesus needed disciples and I suggest that disciples go on needing disciples – firstly, to pass on what we know so that what we know doesn't die, and secondly, to experience friendship along the way. I would say the current crop of younger leaders I am working with are as crazy for the Spirit as any I've worked with. I am relieved and strengthened by that. If we need to send a team anywhere to do anything, I have seven staff members that could do it instead of me. But that does not happen by accident.

What is the price I pay?

I meet some of them individually during the week and all of them together every Sunday evening. Very occasionally, I have to have mildly difficult conversations. Very, very occasionally, I have to end the mentoring relationship because lessons are not being learnt. That's it. What do I get out of it? The joy of seeing people emerge with power, genuine friendship, help in leading the church and new church plants.

Putting other people first

Which leads me to the importance of preferring people and getting out of the way. If someone starts to show all the signs of being able to exercise a gift and we invest in them and they keep on getting better, this should only be seen as a very good thing. We do need to ensure that we continue to use our gifts ourselves, but in general, especially as we get older, we must be committed to blessing what the Spirit is doing in other people. A mature leader is more concerned about influence than impact – though those who are new to leadership and who are younger are going to think a lot about impact and this is OK.

Who can we release into positions of authority so that the work of the Spirit can increase?

The Spirit is always looking to invest in people who seek him. They can suddenly make exponential moves forward, in my experience, and when that happens we need to try and create space for them. Let us be people who bless what God is doing in other people and don't worry about the implications this might have for us. If we make space for other people we will never miss out.

What if they are more gifted than us?

Great, thanks be to God, it's not a competition, we are on the same side, we all win.

A friend once commented after a colleague first spoke at a Carol service, "That was the best carol service talk ever." He was right, but it is worth noting that I had done every other one he had previously heard.

As an evangelist, I have generally led our evangelistic course, the Life Course. But at one stage, I gave away all Life Course leadership and the main evangelistic preaching to my colleague, Ed Flint.

Was it painful? A little bit, but it was mainly joyful to see a truly gifted evangelist emerge and to develop a great friendship with someone who shared the burden of leadership with me. Ultimately, we are getting an amazing church plant out of it.

I remind myself, as I remind you: it was never about us in the first place. It was and is about Jesus, his agenda and his Kingdom. We should aim to raise up as many Kingdom people as we possibly can before we go on to be with the Lord and especially make space for others to emerge as leaders in their own right without fearing for our own ministries.

Dynamics of a time of ministry

Worship

Since our role in the ministry process is to help people to open themselves to God, the quality of the worship in a meeting is very important. Worship was covered in the last chapter, but to recap: the worship experience is like a journey in which we start where people are and hope to move them to a place of openness to God. When we first turn up at something Christian, we are mainly open to ourselves. Questions like, "Am I happy to be here? Who else is here? Do I know anyone?" run through our minds. As we begin to worship, what is on our minds and in our hearts starts to come to the surface and we begin the process of giving things to God/ trying to ignore what is coming up/opening ourselves to God etc.

A gifted worship leader, who can choose the right kinds of songs to help us be truly present at different stages on the journey, can really help increase the power of a time of ministry at the end. It stands to reason that an existing awareness of the presence of the Spirit in the worship leads to more openness to the power of the Spirit when we invite him to come. Therefore, grow in your appreciation and experience of worship. Become aware of what is happening, not just in you but in any given group during worship.

It is no coincidence that some people who are good leaders of ministry have, at one stage, been worship leaders. Testimonies and effective teaching also help with the opening up process, of course.

You

It's not just about them or God, it's also about you as the leader of the time of ministry.

- Have you prayed about what you are about to do? God does nothing but in answer to prayer
- Have you committed your personal concerns and situations to

God and left them with him? We all have stuff going on and sometimes the best we can do is leave it with God and come back to it later. If you wait to resolve everything in your life before you invite the Spirit to come, you won't do that very often.

- Do you feel God has given you something specific? When should it be given? I would ask the Spirit to come first before giving specific words unless they are about who you think should come forward for prayer

- Be aware of your own humanity. Asking the Spirit to come, asking God to do something, exposes you as the leader. A friend of mine once forgot that his microphone was still switched on when, having invited everyone to stand and open themselves to the Spirit, he audibly whispered, "Oh God, I hope this works." Inevitably, in leading something like this, you open yourself up and that means that any anxieties you have about people's perceptions of you or about your "performance" will come shooting up to the surface. I discovered recently that Elvis Presley (a great live performer) never got over stage fright. I have gone through my own version most times I have invited the Spirit to come – especially when praying for non-Christians:

  - what if nothing happens?
  - what if this puts them off?
  - what if I don't know what the Spirit is doing?
  - what if I ask for words of knowledge and no one has any?
  - how can God possibly use me?

The only antidote to this I have found is to feel that I have prayed every prayer I know beforehand. Often, I meet with God during furious times of panic/intercession/anxiety and then gradually come to a place of greater peace. It's easier now than it was. I used to focus on the few people who experienced absolutely nothing in a ministry time when I first started. I have learnt not to do that.

Don't be taken out by what comes up in you.

When we lead ministry (which means "service") we are trying to help others. Refusing to lead when we could or taking it as an opportunity to boast about our spiritual prowess are both evidence of unresolved ego needs. If you don't think your self-worth can stand the challenge of leading ministry, then I have some good news!

It's not your ministry.

Wimber once felt God say to him; "I've seen your ministry John, now let me show you mine." As Paul says, *"Such confidence as this is ours through Christ before God. Not that we are* **competent in ourselves** *to claim anything for ourselves but* **our competence comes from God**. *He has* **made us competent** *as ministers of a new covenant – not of the letter but of the Spirit; for the letter kills but the Spirit gives life"* (2 Corinthians 3:4-6).

Don't make more of your service than it actually is. When people come to church, they come to receive something from God. Quite frankly, it rarely matters to them who is leading worship, speaking or leading ministry – unless that person gets in the way.

Let's try and get over ourselves.

The enemy

Satan isn't a huge fan of anyone seeking to advance the Kingdom of God and he will throw anything available at you to stop you inviting the Spirit to come. He will tempt you to sin, remind you of your failures, state that you will never be any good at this and that you certainly aren't as good as someone else you always compare yourself with. If he can't get you in these ways he may try to buffet you.

I was invited to go to Germany to speak about the Spirit to a community of evangelicals. I was so young and stupid that I didn't realise you needed to arrive early to get on a plane. I thought they were like buses. It occurred to me as I was on the tube that this might not be true. I asked an air stewardess and she told me, "You will have to run." In those days, just after the invention of flight, if you were late you could run to the gate and maybe get on. Just as I was preparing myself to run, a man sitting opposite me started spitting on my suitcase. Then he extracted a large metal bar and started staring at me in a meaningful way.

I shot off the tube – in the wrong direction. He tried to hit me with his bar as I passed him. I dived underneath the bar, like a ninja warrior. I eventually got on the plane. And huge power fell on the Germans.

This will probably never happen to you!

Them

- Are they Christians?
- Are they open to the Spirit?
- Are they theologically opposed? Have you convinced them from the Bible?
- When they look at you, are they seeing someone who did something terrible to them in the past?
- Are they comfortable?
- Do they trust you?
- Are they too hot or too cold?
- Do they understand enough of what is about to happen? Never tell people all the things that could happen; apologise afterwards.
- Do they matter to you?

In so far as we can, our job as leader of the ministry is to help people feel loved and safe from beginning to end. I have found that if I stay visible and calm even during times of great power, people will generally feel OK. But not everyone will and the only way of making the minority feel comfortable is by not asking the Spirit to come. But we can't agree to that. I have sometimes been met with a delegation asking me not to do ministry. I always ignore that if it's been agreed beforehand, sometimes in a nice way.

The Spirit

- Why is he more powerfully present sometimes? (no one really knows).
- What if he's not really doing much that you can see? (that's normal).
- What if you don't know what he's doing? (that's normal).
- Just follow the model. Our job is simply to encourage people to be open by all means available to us. The Holy Spirit then does what he wants to do. He can certainly be limited by how closed people are to him – but he doesn't have to be, obviously. He is God.
- Never say you can see the Spirit doing something if you can't.
- Never the blame the people if not much is happening.
- Never try and whip things up to make yourself feel better.
- Do wait upon the Spirit for as long as you can.

Mechanics

- Leading ministry is very much like praying for one person in that we need to show love, encourage people to open themselves to God, avoid any kind of manipulation, ask the Spirit to come and wait and bless what God is doing.
- I always explain at the start of a service that at the end, we offer to pray for anyone who would like prayer. As we conclude, whoever is leading ministry will recap what the speaker has said about who might like to come forward for prayer, say what they think and/or pick up on prophetic words given earlier. In addition, we always say that anyone who wants prayer for any reason can come forward too.
- If I am leading on the Life Course weekend (when we teach about the Spirit) I will explain that there has been enough

talking from me by this stage and that now it is time to ask God to act. The best way we have found to do this (I explain) is as follows: "In a moment, I'm going to ask us to put away the chairs and find our own personal space on the dance floor – a bit like we did in the gym at school. Then I am going to ask us to open our hands as a symbolic way of saying, 'Hello God, I am open to you' – as opposed to crossing our arms and looking angry, which is a way of saying, 'God, I am not open to you.' No one has to play. The doors are open and you do not have to stay in the room. If you would prefer to watch, you can. All that will happen is that you will stand with your hands open and your eyes closed and there will be a period of silence during which I encourage you to invite the Spirit to come to you. I will add my prayers to yours, that indeed the Spirit will come. Your group leaders will then come and lay hands on you and they will be agreeing with your prayer too. We stand around like that for a while being prayed for. But first, a loo break."

- Encourage people to stand and open their hands and close their eyes, as you would if you were praying for one person.
- Ask the Spirit to come and wait, as you would if praying for one person.
- Invite your team to start praying for people even if you can't see much happening. In my experience, there sometimes isn't much you can see, but still remarkable transformation ensues. Often, their first session of this kind will help people to feel that this is OK and it is only later that they will really open themselves.
- It's great when things immediately start happening, but make sure you explain and reassure as you go along. During the ministry time, I speak gently and calmly and will give public statements of reassurance like, "You are doing very well. I know this is challenging, but I can see that you are trying to open yourselves. I really admire you. Don't be put off by

crying/people falling over/laughing etc. These are just ways in which the Spirit touches people. Don't be afraid. When you hear peoples' stories later, you will understand why they might be expressing themselves like this. I will explain everything in tomorrow's session and you can ask your leaders any questions tonight in the bar."

- It is good if the worship leader plays something in the background so that people can cry if they want to. When people cry I say, "You have to be able to bleed in hospital and cry in church."

- DON'T allow the worship leader to be too loud so you can't hear yourself pray and don't let him or her lead the people back into worship without your permission. When we are opening ourselves to the Spirit, we are seeking to receive; when we are worshipping, we are also giving out.

- Go and pray for people yourself where you can see the Spirit moving, because as things start to happen, the power of God often increases in the room.

- Do share the leadership of the ministry if you can.

- Watch for waves of power in which God is doing the same thing in several people. Draw attention to this so that those being touched realise it is God and see if others can "catch" what is happening.

- Afterwards, dialogue with your team, hear about their experiences and talk about yours.

- Do something to relax because, especially to start with, ministering to people is exhausting.

- Be careful not to fall into sin. It is so weird for us to walk in the Spirit, to be used by God, that we can panic and look for something familiar – like the sad old patterns of the flesh.

Build A Ministry Team
Once you are used to praying for people individually and in groups,

the next obvious step is to train other people to do what you do.

- Once again, we are called to be disciples of Jesus. How did he spend most of his time? Not engaging with social issues or creating authentic community or being nice. He preached the Gospel, healed the sick and cast out demons. What did the first disciples spend their time doing? The same. Obviously, all Christians are not called to do this on a full-time basis. The majority are called to work in the world. But I believe that all Christian should be taught how to minister to people in the power of the Spirit. You will find that some people absolutely love it. Teach them as much as you can.
- Model that you think praying for people in the power of the Spirit is a priority. We pray for people in most of our meetings and at virtually all of our services. All churches always get what they preach for and conversely they do not get what they do not preach for. This is rule number one of church leadership.
- Once ministry is established, share leadership as quickly as you can. Give away as much as you can so that others can grow. Continue to monitor how your leaders are doing. Don't simply delegate and leave.
- Train your people. Encourage as many people as possible to be involved, but make it clear that they need to be equipped and authorised. To be authorised you have to share in the vision and values of ministry. This allows for accountability. If people want to minister with a different theology or model they can't do it in your church and claim to represent it.
- Those who are interested should sign up for training. We train people twice a year. All those who have trained will now be expected to pray for others at the end of services. However, sometimes the Spirit is doing something in them and they have to be allowed to receive as well.
- Do ministry as you train others – don't just talk about it – and

leave room for questions.

- Publicly authorise new team members and identify them in some way when they pray in church. Lack of experience doesn't matter that much and neither does lack of confidence; both of these things will change over time. What does matter is theology that seriously clashes with yours or practices that differ from your model. A critical absence of personal wholeness or interpersonal skills also matters. Would you be happy to have so-and-so pray for your friend? Bite the bullet where you have concerns and do not authorise unsuitable people to pray or you will be storing up trouble for later when people complain.

- Stress the team's accountability to you, but don't claim infallibility: "I'm in charge because someone has to determine the guidelines and the model, but we can always discuss what's going on. Maybe I'll change my mind about this or that."

- Praying in pairs is good to start with, a more experienced person with a less experienced one.

- Always have someone visible who is in charge of a ministry time as a point of reference and also, someone who can step in to a situation if necessary.

- Invite others with more experience into your setting so that everyone can grow in their experience of the Spirit.

- If you are ever invited to speak somewhere and pray for people, always try and take others with you.

- Normalise the whole thing in your setting in so far as you can; have prophecies, give words of knowledge, encourage stories about what God has done, pray at the end of services and in most other contexts.

If you can establish a culture in which ministry in the Spirit is normal, you too will have the joy of seeing all the wonderful works of God. That's the best thing ever.

True story

"I had been a Christian for 22 years and in full-time ministry for almost 15 years. I was in a seminary and church that taught all the supernatural gifts of the Holy Spirit had ceased. However, in ministry and my own relationship with Jesus I was tired, discouraged and felt disconnected from him.

I was invited over to a Life Course weekend run by St Mary's. I was told that it was a weekend to learn about and experience the Holy Spirit. I was excited, but also hesitant, because of what I had been taught about the gifts of the Spirit having ceased. But I read a book before I went which convinced me that all the gifts of the Holy Spirit were available for believers today.

When the opportunity came to wait on the Holy Spirit, I was expectant but terrified. I stood with my arms open, eyes closed and heart beating out of my chest. I wasn't sure what was going to happen. I literally thought I might fly across the room. But I was open and wanting everything God had for me. Someone began to pray for me and I crumbled, gently falling to the ground, feeling the Father's love wash over me. The weight of his love was such that I could not move. I was experiencing his love in a way that I never had before through the Holy Spirit. I stayed there for so long and didn't want to get up. I probably could have, but I remember thinking, 'I don't want to move and lose or stop what I am feeling.'

My best friend, who came with me, also had a powerful encounter. We couldn't believe that we had gone so long as Christians and never experienced the Holy Spirit. We called our wives and they thought we had either gone crazy, were smoking crack or had just joined a cult.

During the next time of ministry, I forced myself to get off the ground and look at what was happening. People of all races, all ages praying for one another. I thought, 'This is what heaven will be like' and, 'I want to lead a church like this.'

That would have been incredible in itself, but it turned out to be only the beginning. My family moved to London so that I could learn how to minister in the power of the Spirit before leading a church plant from St Mary's in the place I live.

Over the years, God has used us to bring emotional, spiritual and physical healing to many people. God has moved particularly powerfully in those who have a misunderstanding about the Father's love for them, because of some kind of abuse that has occurred in their life. We have also seen people healed of cancer, hepatitis, mental illness and other diseases that are incurable. We attracted people that other churches did not accept, or who were made to feel second class. One person said, 'Your church is the church you go to if you are messed up.' We have planted two churches with these same values and continue to have a vision to plant more."

About the Author

 John Peters is Rector of St Mary, Bryanston Square, an Anglican church in central London. Over the years the church has grown as John and others have sought to communicate the Gospel in a culturally relevant way. St Mary's has also planted several churches in the UK and abroad with similar vision and values. John is married to Jenny and they have three children, Josh, Zoe and Natasha.